D1516519

PSYCHOLOGICAL DOG TRAINING

BEHAVIOR CONDITIONING
with
RESPECT AND TRUST

by

C.W. MEISTERFELD

Cover Art by T. Bruce
Illustrations by Charlotte J. Schriber
Edited by Heidi Steinmueller

M R K PUBLISHING

The Publishing House truly dedicated to Man's Best Friend

Library of Congress Catalogue
No. 90-092084

ISBN 0-9601292-6-X

M R K PUBLISHING
448 Seavey
PETaluma, CA 94952
(707) 763-0056

Typeset by A-to-Z Word Processing, Sebastopol, California, U.S.A.
Printed by Patterson Printing, Benton Harbor, Michigan, U.S.A.

DEAR DOG OWNER:

- If you want your dog to develop his own behavior don't train him.

- Respond always obediently to all of his demands and grant him any freedom he desires, the run of the house, the yard, the property, and other areas.

- Never require him to do anything for you.

- Don't be surprised if he barks excessively, digs, chews, chases whatever moves, soils your house, destroys your furniture, **threatens you and bites, or even attacks your child.**

However, if you don't want to tolerate these typical and normal dog behavior traits, **you must teach your dog a different behavior which is acceptable to you.**

You have to educate him in a way which is pleasant for him and where no confrontation and fear is involved. **Your dog should learn to respect you but not to be afraid of you.**

You should not condition and reinforce his instinctive behaviors and activities which disturb you. For instance, if you don't want him to chew on your shoes or carpet, don't buy him lots of chew toys. He should only be permitted to chew on his food, e.g., a big bone. If you don't want him to chase joggers and bikers, don't let him run freely in parks, fields, and at the beach. If you don't want him to bite, don't roughhouse with him. The more you condition him to use his teeth, the more is he apt to bite.

Training should start immediately, when you bring your new puppy or an older dog home. Remember, as his owner, you are responsible for your dog's behavior in every respect, even legally. Without training, your dog has only his instinctive behaviors, many of which are unacceptable and very dangerous, such as biting.

Since you provide everything for your dog and your dog is completely dependent on you, **you have to set the rules and limits according to your needs, and your dog has to obey them.** Thus, you must be his master and authority figure but never his subordinate and servant.

The best way to establish yourself as your dog's master is to have this attitude of responsibility and to obedience-train him with psychological methods.

C.W. Meisterfeld

TABLE OF CONTENTS

C.W. MEISTERFELD is a professional canine psychoanalyst/
therapist with over 35 years experience in the dog world. His many
awards include the National Retriever Championship (perfect 500
score) and Canine Distinction Award for A.K.C. obedience. Since
1963 he has pioneered the concept and practice of canine psycho-
analysis and psychological training using only positive reinforcement. His books are published internationally. One of his books
(Tails of a Dog Psychoanalyst) received an award for excellence by
the Dog Writers' Association of America. He teaches canine
behavioral psychology at colleges and universities, is a California
Superior Court qualified canine behavior analyst, and a member of
the National Speakers Association.

DEDICATION

This book is dedicated to all the dog owners and dog trainers who desire to learn how to **TRAIN WITH PLEASURE, NOT PAIN.** Also, to "to Man's Best Friend" who I pray will forgive Man's Ignorance.

GRATITUDE

from the depth of my heart and soul to one and all who contributed to this creation.
And especially to those who **stood up to be counted** with their **CONFESSIONS** and **TESTIMONIES.**

'The Dog Whisperer'

For more information contact our Web page

at WWW.DOGWHISPER.COM

MAN'S BEST FRIEND IS LOSING HIS IMAGE! WHY?

It took over 3,000 years of selective breeding to create the characteristics in our domestic dogs we value so much. We have bred them for certain tasks, purposes, and performances. We imprinted in them genetically their friendliness and loyalty toward mankind and their willingness to work for us and please us.

Still 40 years ago dogs were reliable, sociable, amiable animals eagerly working for us and serving our needs. Dog fights and bites were an exception. Even small children could be left alone with the family dog without any harmful consequences.

When I was extensively travelling the Eastern States and the Midwest attending field, water, and obedience trials during the '50s and '60s, never once did I see dog fights or a dog expressing aggressive behavior toward people. Dogs used to respect not only humans but also each other.

Yet in the past year I witnessed at six dog shows several incidents of dog aggression toward other dogs and people. I consider this very alarming.

Why is the dog not anymore what he used to be, and when did his deterioration start?

Forceful Dominant Training Techniques

In the wake of the Back-to-Nature trend in the early '70s the idea to imitate canine behavior for conditioning and controlling our domestic dogs was presented to the public by leading animal behaviorists. This concept of people and dogs interrelating as the "pack" on an animal level was very well received and generally adopted.

The majority of dog training books and dog training institutions recommend dominant techniques in combination with the display of extensive affection toward the dog as the *non plus ultra* of dog training. This is taught throughout the U.S.

Although, this approach works with some dogs, the majority of behaviorally disturbed, aggressive, vicious dogs that dog owners brought to me for testing and evaluating were conditioned with "natural" forceful-dominant methods.

The following facts reflect an alarming development:

- The number of dog problems and bites has been soaring. In 1980 1 million was reported and in 1989 over 3 million. That equates to 8,200 dog bites reported every day throughout the U.S. According to the Humane Society of the U.S., the number of unreported bites is up to 40 times higher. That adds up to approximately 120 million dog bites a year and over 300,000 bites a day! This sounds hard to believe, but I have had owners consulting me whose dog bit them several times a week and who had scars all over their hands, arms and legs.

- The number of small children attacked and killed by dogs of "friendly breeds" for no apparent reasons is increasing.

- More and more dogs are being destroyed because of behavior problems (approximately 13 million in 1989). I know of four A.K.C. champion dogs of various breeds from the San Francisco/ Bay Area who were put down this summer because of their sudden vicious Dr. Jekyll/Mr. Hyde behavior. All four of them had been conditioned with forceful-dominant methods.

The irony is that dominant methods are generally described and offered to the public as "non-violent," although they are based on physical force and aggression (controlling through fear) to be exercised by the dog owner/trainer toward the dog.

Since it is relatively easy to throw a young, small puppy on his back when applying the Alpha Roll-Over, and also to grab the pup on the scruff of his neck and shake him hard several times, or to hit him forcefully under the chin until he yelps, this becomes more and more difficult and eventually impossible with on older and full-grown dog. Many mature dogs will not tolerate this treatment anymore from their owners or trainers and will express their disapproval with growling and finally a bite. (See *JELLY BEAN VS...*)

Perhaps you had a similar experience with your dog, such as Chris Biggins of San Francisco with her German Shepherd Innis.

Innis

Innis was enrolled in a Puppy Kindergarten Training class, in order to be socialized and learn the basics of obedience. He graduated as one of the top dogs in the class. Chris was very pleased with him and thought she was well on her way to having a happy, obedient and well-trained dog. The only problem was that she had a difficult time getting Innis to stop chewing on her hand and clothes. She assumed that was just a puppy teething problem and he would outgrow this. Also, he did not obey all the time, only when he felt like it.

At ten months of age, Innis growled at Chris' husband when he tried to take a toy away from him. They disciplined him by shaking him, yelling at him, and for good measure, doing the alpha roll-over that they had learned in the PKT class. According to what they had read and been taught, if they did a good enough job of disciplining, the aggressive episodes would not recur.

Unfortunately, it did not work that way. Innis growled at them several more times for which they punished him heavily in the usual way. It seemed that every time they did this, Innis got worse. He continued to growl at them, began to get into fights with other dogs, and also started to growl at people and dogs walking by their house.

Finally, one day after Chris had disciplined him again, Innis attacked her and managed to bite her hand. Since punishment did not seem to work, Chris and her husband had a consultation with an animal behaviorist. They were told that Innis probably had a genetic defect, and that they should neuter him. They did not do so because they wanted to breed him. Also, they did not think this was the problem.

The situation got worse. Innis bit Chris again when she scolded him, this time more severely. Now they realized that the problem had gotten out of hand.

Fortunately, Chris came across *JELLY BEAN VS...* at a local dog show and learned from this book the reason for Innis' behavior problem and that there is an alternative, positive solution to it—Psychological Training.

Modern Puppy Socialization and Training Classes
(Puppy Kindergarten Training Classes)

Puppy Socialization Classes became the hit of the '80s and are very popular everywhere. Basically, their program consists of a great amount of uncontrolled, playful interaction of the puppies along with an obedience training period.

Scores of immature little puppies are thrown together to "socialize" in order to "support the development of a healthy, normal social behavior and a sound temper," as videos, books and other advertising material promise.

The delighted owners of young puppies watch how their pets indulge in romping, chasing and biting each other playfully. This does not require any effort of the dog owners. It also looks cute and is quite entertaining.

Because experts made them believe so, these owners are convinced that by "socializing" their puppies nothing can go wrong anymore with the behavior of their maturing dog, and that they will now have a sound-tempered dog.

However, the continued uncontrolled, free interactions of the puppies practiced in these classes can increase the flaws in their personality makeup.

I totally agree with the general concept of early puppy training and think it has great virtues.

When I was breeding German Shorthair Pointers and Black Labs in the '50s and '60s, I would take the whole litter of pups at four to five weeks, who were not yet weaned (leaving the mother at home), over to the field and shallow water to evaluate the extent of their hunting instinct

12

and condition them. I trained them to follow me and to respond to directional changes and whistle signals. They learned fast and performed beautifully. Later on, after they were well-trained, I socialized them with strange dogs and people without any subsequent problems.

If we look at the scenario of a Puppy Kindergarten Puppy Class the following becomes obvious:

By encouraging the pups to run-play, wrestle together, pinning one another down (the alpha roll-over), and to bite each other, we actually support the conditioning of a primitive aggressive-dominant behavior. The playing of dogs with each other is always a practicing of aggressive dominance: Who is stronger? And they use their teeth to prove it.

THESE DOGS ARE CONSIDERED

Photo by permission of Annie Wells

The Press Democrat, Santa Rosa, California

THESE DOGS ARE CONSIDERED PLAYING AND HAVING FUN!

(1) The Wrestling Aggressive Dogs
(2) The Misguided Dog Owner
(3) The Serious Potential Attacker
(4) The Innocent Potential Victim
(5) The Unsuspecting Mother

This picture depicts very aggressive dog behavior. Note the dogs' threatening body language. The dominant dog's stiff tail as he stands over the submissive one focusing on his throat shows that he meant business.

The intensity of the white dog's eye, his erect ears, his head and neck angled and stiff, his slightly opened mouth and curled lips reflect that he was keyed to attack. All he needed was to get free and to prove that he was top dog.

Since the child was very close, it could have become involved, and this "fun play" could have ended as a tragedy adding another victim to the list of the 1990 dog bite fatalities—mainly children.

It would serve our puppies well to learn and practice (with their teeth) to establish their ranking position and help their survival, if they would be living in a wild dog pack. Here, physical dominance is a crucial issue since the social interactions of the pack members are based on it. Only the strongest animal can be the pack leader and control the pack. As such, he has to respond to permanent challenges and must fight to maintain his position. He will remain the pack leader only as long as no other pack member is stronger than him.

Since our pups are not living in a dog pack in the wilds but in a civilized human family, they do not need to be dominant and challenging or further their survival with physical force. On the contrary, if they express dominant behavior, which they typically demonstrate with their teeth, they even endanger their survival. It is a sad truth that many biting dogs are being put down.

Many owners experience in the training part of their KPT class that their pup is so charged up by all these preceding activities and challenges that it wants to continue the playful part by biting the owner's hands and

16

feet, by jumping up on the owner, trying to bite the back of the owner's legs, etc. Also, it is not very eager to work and please.

The consequence is that the puppy then is punished for this behavior which was permitted and encouraged 15 minutes earlier. Typical instructions from trainers are to reprimand the pup, if it does not obey, by jerking on its collar, by slapping it hard under the chin, etc.

As an essential element of puppy training the owner is instructed to establish himself as the pack leader by practicing dominant techniques on his pup, such as scruff-shaking it, suspending it on its front legs in the air and shaking it hard, throwing the pup on the back and pinning it down, to name a few examples.

Thus, after by its playmates, the puppy is being further conditioned in an aggressive dominant way, now by human beings.

Besides the cruelty, nobody seems ever have thought about the health hazards of a scruff-shake. By shaking the puppy very hard as advised, not only **brain damage** can result (hemorrhage) but also **spinal and neck problems**.

There are many cases of small children documented who were brain-damaged from heavy shaking. Some even died. Why should a puppy be more resistant to violent shaking than a small child?

What are we doing to our dogs? We do not want dominant dogs, but we do everything to create them by condition them with dominant methods. Then, when they exhibit dominant behavior, as a result of their continued dominant conditioning, we punish and eventually euthanize them.

It is the dog that suffers in the long run when he must be destroyed.

This whole concept just does not make sense. Until a large-scale national educational program is presented to the approximately 60 million dog owners in the U.S. rectifying the misconceptions, there will be more dog bites, related fatalities, and decimation of dogs. Consequently, by the year 2000 not many families will be able to own a dog anymore.

Many of the behaviorally disturbed dogs which are brought to me for testing and reprogramming are socialized, owner-dominated puppies.

One of these examples, is Darby, a beautiful Kerry Blue Terrier, who belongs to the breeder Kathi Stidwell (now one of my disciples) of Castro Valley, California.

Darby

At the age of three months Darby exhibited signs of shyness. To overcome this behavior, Kathi followed expert advice and took Darby to a puppy training and socialization class. In addition, she walked the puppy in shopping centers and around loud noises to "desensitize" him as recommended.

When the dog was eight months old she started an obedience class with Darby. Darby showed so much fear in class that it was difficult to work him. The trainer immediately told Kathy, "Your dog is so fearful around other dogs because he hasn't been socialized!"

This was too much for Kathi. She had Darby extensively checked regarding his health and behavior by a California Veterinarian College.

Kathi was told that the dog was fine, that she should continue to expose him to all the noises and situations which bothered him, in order to further desensitize him. And, if that would not work, she might consider putting Darby on Valium.

The dog continued to grow worse and became almost paranoid with fear.

Kathi contacted me for psychological testing and evaluation.

After six weeks of reprogramming with psychological methods, Darby, an extremely intelligent and sensitive dog, lost his fear and started on his way to recovery to a normal, happy dog.

Darby's case history and others show what effect puppy socialization classes in their present form can have on the behavior development of puppies. Fearful puppies can become more fearful, and aggressive puppies can practice their assertiveness and willfulness on the subservient ones.

Most puppies who come to PKT classes have not yet received any prior training. They have not learned that there are territorial and behavioral boundaries to observe. Their mind has not yet been structured in a disciplined way through training. They are completely unprepared for this new situation to which they are exposed. They are being confronted with lots of strange people and lots of other puppies which can become overwhelming for them. They cannot but respond to this challenge on their basic level, the level of survival, i.e., flight or fight, depending on their individual personalities. Their primitive instincts are being further strengthened.

Through this kind of socialization, a sensitive and shy puppy will not miraculously transform into a bold dog and an aggressive puppy will not become placid, as case histories prove. Their basic personalities will not only not change at all but become more manifest in the long run.

I am consulting with other dog owners who attended PKT classes, where their pups scored high in the tests. They were very much surprised when their dog suddenly started to defy their commands, snarled, growled, and even bit, if they did not back off.

From experts they got the answer that their dog is just going through an adolescent stage and that he should not be permitted to get away with it but beaten down.

I really feel sorry for these poor dogs. Through the permissiveness of letting the dogs form their own behavior responses toward other dogs, people and things, the dogs were put in charge. Their territorial boundaries were not defined by their owners.

With the development of the will-to-power (supported by the dominant behavior conditioning) and by neglecting the reinforcement of the will-to-serve based on establishing respect and trust, the dog has no choice but to express his dominant position in the pecking order with his natural means — his teeth.

We systematically eradicate Man's Best Friend's friendliness and devotion toward us by conditioning him first with overpermissiveness and self-gratification and then with fear and coercion through dominance and punishment concepts. In addition, we overburden him with our overflowing emotions. Since he is "only" a dog, he cannot handle this conflict without any adverse reactions.

Dominant conditioning based on fear triggers the dog's survival instinct and an adrenal surge. Using the dog as the object of our powerful human emotional needs exceeds his mental limits. Being too permissive

19

and inconsistent frustrates him. As a consequence, he exhibits neurotic behavior. His adrenal glands are stimulated in an undesired way (See *JELLY BEAN VS...*).

Even noted friendly breeds now increasingly exhibit willful and violent behavior not only toward strangers but also toward family members.

Lack of Training

The dog's genetically imprinted will-to-serve-and-please mankind has been reinforced and utilized through special training over centuries. For example, working dogs were put through a strict training program to enable them to fulfill their specific task.

On the level of servitude and respect the dog is happy and knows his position. He does not need to use his teeth to reinforce it.

Today, instead of developing the dog's will-to-serve and respect toward the owner through psychological training and structuring the mind, many dogs are given various privileges in the family and lots of physical exercise by turning them loose and permitting them to run free on the beach or in parks.

This is pure self-gratification for the dog. His assertive will-to-power, which he enforces with the usage of his teeth, is strengthened and his adrenal flow stimulated. Ruling the family and running sprees highly condition his primitive instincts and reduce him to the level of his wild ancestors — to be self-governed, self-directed and self-gratified.

II.

WHAT YOU SHOULD KNOW BEFORE
YOU START TRAINING

The purpose of this book is to fulfill an urgent need and respond to the requests of the readers of my preceding book, *JELLY BEAN VS. DR. JEKYLL & MR. HYDE—Written for the SAFETY of our CHILDREN & the WELFARE of our DOGS*, to learn more in detail about the mechanics of my psychological dog training and reprogramming concepts.

This book replaces my first book *HOWS & WHYS OF PSYCHO-LOGICAL DOG TRAINING* published in 1977.

Many readers of *JELLY BEAN VS...* expressed that it was a revelation to learn about the existence of the successful alternative of psychologically training and reprogramming dogs instead of using the dominant concepts of physical force and punishment.

They also admitted that they did not feel good with the approach they were taught in training classes and by the books. Despite their great efforts to prove to their dog who is the boss by shaking him, throwing him down and rolling him over, their dog grew worse.

Unfortunately, some of these owners had to put their dominant-conditioned dog down when he started to dominate and threaten them and became too dangerous to be around. They did not know then that they could have saved the dog.

Perhaps you have also experienced that the force-punishment-submission system did not work with your dog, and you had to discard your pet.

Since establishing physical dominance is gospel for the "dog world," it is no surprise that statistics reflect an annual increase of dog problems and bites.

21

After devoting over 25 years of my life to testing and working with problem dogs to understand why the once friendly family puppy suddenly turns into a Dr. Jekyll & Mr. Hyde, I have arrived at the realization that Konrad Lorenz' statement, "The most violent form of fighting behavior is motivated by fear," is a truism. VIOLENCE BEGETS VIOLENCE!!!

I consider the dogma that dogs can only be perfectly controlled by humans with physical dominance a degradation of Man's Best Friend and an insult to his evolutionary development. In my opinion, advocating these animalistic methods is also a disgrace to mankind.

To help you to have a pleasant, problem-free relationship with your dog I offer you a new kind of training approach without the need to physically establish dominance. The formula is **PSYCHOLOGICAL DOG TRAINING—CONDITIONING WITH RESPECT AND TRUST**.

PSYCHOLOGICAL DOG TRAINING is not composed of miracle commands or magic words. However, it provides you with a new philosophy which will certainly work "like magic" with your dog when you follow it to the letter.

My psychological training system is very simple and can be practiced by everybody. It consists of efficiently and positively communicating with the dog and structuring his mind based on respect and trust.

With psychological methods I have been able to successfully train and reprogram more than 3,000 dogs in the past 35 years. Many of them were several years old and had very serious behavior problems. Some were considered incurable.

The owners of these dogs experienced for the first time that their dogs bonded with them and expressed devotion and loyalty.

Bonding

There seems to be a great deal of misunderstanding regarding the bonding of a dog with his owner.

Bonding is not just an abstract emotional principle but it finds its expression in the devoted and loyal attachment of the dog to his owner and vice versa.

Does a dog bond with his owner when he is acquired as a very young puppy, if he is cared for, catered to, and loved dearly?

If this would be the case, most of the millions of dog owners would be very happy with their pets, since these conditions are usually met. There would be no owner-dog-problem relationships.

I have consulted with hundreds of dog owners who got their pup at an early age, spoiled their pet in every respect with special cooking, the best food, with all amenities and creature comfort. They even let the dog decide who would be permitted to come into the house. These owner just loved their dog to death.

Yet the dog did not reciprocate. Instead, he started to growl and bite, if the owner wanted him to do something the dog disliked, such as getting him off the sofa, etc.

In fact, most of the reported and unreported dog bites take place in the home by the family dog. As the American Medical Association in THE HARVARD MEDICAL SCHOOL HEALTH LETTER states, from the over 44,000 facial bites mainly inflicted on children, 96% are unprovoked and brought on by the family dog.

This behavior can really not be considered as an expression of bonding. The opposite is true.

How and when does a dog bond with his owner?

In the experts' opinion, bonding between dog and owner basically takes place in the early stages of the puppy's life.

If the bonding period would be limited to a certain time frame, it would not be possible to adopt a several years old dog from the Humane Society and enjoy a happy relationship with him. Also, my clients, whose three to four year old dogs I successfully reprogrammed, would not have experienced for the first time devotion and loyalty from their pets.

Among them was an even older dog, a 10 year old yellow Cocker Spaniel, who had been biting the owner and his wife for nine and a half years. He had also attacked mail carriers.

Yet just after eight weeks of psychological training, solely done by his owner who used the principles you are about to read, a complete behavior change occurred in the dog. Max bonded for the first time in 10 years with his owner and never bit again. The mail was once again delivered to their home.

This case history and all the others prove that dogs can bond at any age with any owner whom they respect and trust. The secret for bonding and loyalty is the development of the dog's genetically imprinted will-to-serve-and-please. This can only be accomplished if no physical dominance and other forceful techniques are used when interrelating with the dog.

THERE IS HOPE THAT YOUR DOG WILL BOND WITH YOU WHEN YOU USE THE PROPER APPROACH—PSYCHOLOGICAL TRAINING CONCEPTS BASED ON THE FOUNDATION OF RESPECT.

I respect even the most vicious dog who comes through my door, and I do not challenge or threaten him. I know he was not born vicious. His behavior is just an effect of his environmental conditioning. To be non-judgmental and non-aggressive is the key to dealing with aggressive and fearful dogs and changing their behavior.

This attitude of respect and non-aggressiveness is the cornerstone of my training philosophy with which I lay the foundation for a new positive behavior in the dog. By teaching the dog the commands with respect, instead of using physical dominance applied as force, pain and punishment, the dog will learn to respect me. Thanks to this consistent positive treatment the dog will develop trust in me.

Thus, the preconditions for reaching the training apex are established—the dog expressing his awakening and steadily growing will-to-serve-and-please which will then elevate to loyalty.

The will-to-serve has been inbred and imprinted in our dogs for thousands of years during the domestication process. Unfortunately, it is being systematically destroyed by forceful-dominant training or no training at all.

Based on the description and understanding of dog behavior contained in *JELLY BEAN VS...*, I will explain the mechanics of psychological dog training in a step-by-step course to build your training pyramid.

If you have a young puppy with no former training and no obvious problems, I recommend that you read through the book first and then start to practice the suggested exercises a week at a time. If your pup is a slow learner, you should consider more time for each exercise.

If you have already trained your dog with dominant techniques and thus conditioned behavior problems, please realize that it will take longer than an 8-week course to re-establish the bond of respect and trust between you and your pet.

You should consider that your dog formed his negative behavior over a period of time, sometimes over years. Because of the Memory-Relationship-Responses, and depending on the extent of your own personal changes in the relationship with your dog, the reprogramming process will take a while.

I recommend to extend each weekly exercise to ten to twelve days. Then, as you increase your dog's learning ability, to drop back to the seven-day week. This will take place by the third or fourth week. **Remember, make haste slowly**.

Once you interrelate with your dog on the basis of mutual respect and trust and without aggression you can change his attitude and re-awaken and cultivate his will-to-serve-and-please and his loyalty toward you. His behavior problems will disappear, even very serious ones and problems with older dogs.

Like a mirror image, the dog's attitude and behavior will reflect your own.

PLEASE REMEMBER, YOU CAN AVOID DOG BEHAVIOR PROBLEMS BY NOT CONDITIONING THEM.

III.

THE 10 COMMANDMENTS . . . FOR DOG OWNERSHIP
TO PREVENT BEHAVIOR PROBLEMS

1. Before you buy that cute, fluffy puppy, make sure you are able to fulfill the responsibilities of dog ownership.

2. If you do not plan to breed your dog, have him/her neutered while young, in order not to contribute to the creation of more unwanted dogs which have to be destroyed.

3. You have to train your dog and establish his behavioral and physical boundaries. Like children, dogs are not born with a set of good manners.

4. Do not use abusive, cruel, dominant training methods. As you give shall you receive.

5. Start training with psychological concepts when your dog is three to four months old, in some cases even earlier.

6. Remain non-judgmental when training. Otherwise, you trigger your admonitions to punish.

7. Make haste slowly. Only repetition and patience will produce a well-mannered dog. Never overwork your dog.

8. Be always consistent. Nothing is more detrimental to your dog's positive behavior development than inconsistency.

9. Do not humanize your dog. He walks on four legs.

10 God granted you stewardship over the animal kingdom. Thus, it is up to you to decide who is in charge . . . you? or your dog?

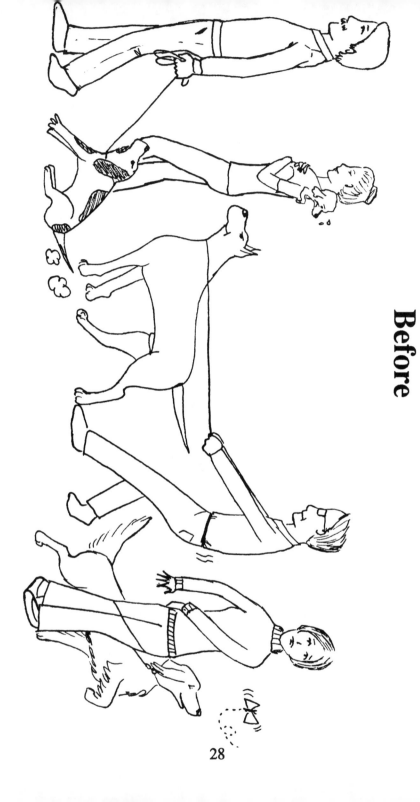

Before

IV.

Psychological Training Begins

FIRST WEEK

- Forward

- Gotcha Zone

- Loose Leash

- Heel

- About Turn

- Timing

- Memory Relationship Response

Come right into the kennel. That's it. And bring your owners
with you.

Please form around the training ring. Don't bunch up—keep your dogs apart!

My training methods are a product of my philosophy and experiences. We will learn the mechanics of basic obedience along with understanding and experiencing how this affects the mental/ emotional make-up of both your dog and yourself. Will-to-power, fear conditioning, temperament and emotions will be some of the subjects covered.

As far as pure breeds versus mongrels are concerned, there is no difference in training. Mentally and emotionally they react and operate the same way. Neither one is superior regarding the learning abilities. You can own a willing pure breed as well as a willing mutt.

We do not want to overwork our dogs even not in class. Therefore, I will be talking more than you will be walking. The instructions will be progressive so it will be absolutely necessary to attend class every week. Practice the exercises daily. If per chance you run into a training problem at home, don't force it. Bring it up in the next class. It's possible other owners are having the same experience. Feel free to ask questions during our breaks. Understanding is needed before progress can be made.

We will do left heel training, which means that your dog will walk on your left side. The class will start off each week going around the training ring in a counter-clockwise direction. My position will be in the center of the ring. At times, when you need individual instructions, I will call your name which I should know by next week. When you need individual help as you are working your dog, I may handle him for a couple of minutes. Remember, this is progressive and if there is something you do not fully understand, ask.

To make sure that each individual and its dogs move in unison with the class, I will give you certain commands. The word **"forward"** is used to start the class off walking. The loop end of the leash is held in your right hand, the left hand holding the leash alongside your left thigh. Leave a few inches of slack when walking. The training ring is so designed that you can turn at the corners without any commands from me.

For the first few times when you start off, do not give any commands or corrections to your dogs. Just encourage them as you walk. **You can catch more flies with honey than you can with vinegar**. While you're walking, pat your left thigh and say, "That's a good girl. That's a good boy. *Good* girl. *Good* boy. That's it. Boy o boy!"

Repeat one of these phrases or something similar every 4 or 5 steps you take. By doing this you will develop their attention span. A three of four second attention span is needed in order for your dog to absorb the training. Otherwise he's like a child gazing out of the classroom window not hearing a thing the teacher is saying. So be sure to keep their attention.

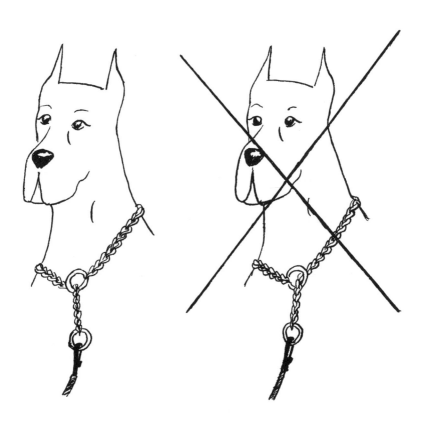

Before we begin our training, let's make sure the chain collar is on the right way. I will come around and check. With the chain on the proper way, it will loosen itself around the dog's neck after you pulled on it and then released it. This action is done lightly and quickly; a snap-release. I will call this action "snapl." Now, when putting the chain on the improper way (that is the leash ring coming from under the neck instead of over the top), it has a choke effect. When you release the chain, it does not loosen up.

Are you ready? Have your dogs on your left side and keep 10 to 12 feet behind the person in front of you.

Let's all face in a counter-clockwise direction.

Forward.

No commands, just encouragement.

Don't be afraid to talk to them.

Try not to stop.

We will walk around the training ring for a few minutes.

Stop.

Relax. Talk to your dog. Give him a pat or two. This is as new to him as it is to you.

Next time, to initiate a stop, you I will use the word "halt."

Let's start again.

Forward.

That's the way. "Here boy, here girl." Pat your thigh as you step off. For those whose dogs are pulling, the next exercise will help you. Once more around the ring.

Halt.

Let's break in place for a minute. Any questions?

Jackie - Why is a leather leash required over a chain leash, and why does it have to be six feet long?"

Trainer - Leather is easier on your hands, especially when we get into further exercises. The six foot length allows the handler to be that far away from the dog, yet still have physical control over him when needed. The six feet are also the border edge of the Gotcha Zone.

Susan - Gotcha Zone! What's that?

Trainer - It is the area within 5 to 8 feet where the dog senses you can reach him physically. Outside this range he knows, you *can't* reach him physically. Have you ever seen some dogs come only so close to the owner when called, but would not come any closer? They are reluctant to enter the "Gotcha Zone."

GOTCHA ZONE

Let's do some more work.

Forward. Walk them gently.

Give them some encouragement and a treat.

That's better. Your dogs are more calm now.

Halt.

The next exercise is the about turn. This is a very good maneuver for the pulling, leading dogs. Just when they think they know where you are going, you change directions. This lets them know that *you* are in control of the walk.

As you are walking, I will say "about turn," at which time you put your left foot forward, pivot on the ball of the foot and turn to your right doing a 180 degree turn. Now you are going back from where you came.

Forward.

Keep up the encouragement. As Plato, the philosopher, said, "Early learning should be pleasurable." Now I am going to give the command for you to turn around. Remember, left foot, and turn to your right.

About turn.

That's the way, just keep walking in the clockwise direction.

Halt.

I saw a few of you jerking your dogs on the about turn. Using this method will only sour them to training. You *do not* want to physically turn them around, just signal them. In the beginning, when you turn and your dog is still going the other way, pause until he reaches the end of the leash. When he looks your way say, "Hey, where are you going? I'm going this way," and start walking. When he catches up to you say, "Good boy, good girl." You have a question?

Mary - Why are we starting out using sentences for walking and turning around instead of giving the "heel" command?

Trainer - Because we want to take Plato's advice and introduce the training to our dogs on an enjoyable level. This is why you do not jerk on your dog in the beginning, so that any displeasure he feels at the moment will not be associated with the word "heel."

For instance, can you imagine how willing a dog would be to work if he was jerked every time he heard the word "heel?" And when doing an about turn he gets yet another "heel" and a jerk? It sure can make a happy, willing, working dog just the opposite. He could very well become a problem in training.

Mary - Thank you.

Any more questions?

While you are walking, keep your eyes on your dog, your ears on me.

Forward.

Just your normal walk. Encourage them.

About turn.

That's it. Praise when they catch up.

Halt.

We now have three exercises. From the appearance, one more time around and they will be ready to receive their first command. So, once more.

Forward.

About turn.

Halt.

The dogs are shaping up great. Let's teach them a command for all this.

Now "heel" does not necessarily mean movement. It means only to keep their right shoulder parallel with your left thigh. Have 3 to 4 inches of slack in the leash.

Slack Leash

The loose leash will be helpful in training your dog to walk with you without a leash; or what is called "offleash" work. It also allows him enough leeway to turn corners, or do about turns.

Are we all ready? Dogs on your left side. When I say "forward" to you, you say, "heel" to your dog. Use loose leashes. *Do not use the name*, only the "heel" command.

Forward.

About turn.

About turn.

Halt.

I saw several of you jerking the leash when you stepped off. We do not want to teach the dog that "heel" means a jerk on his neck. Remember, this will only condition a slow, unhappy working dog. Don't forget "Plato" and the "Fly." Here we go. Be sure to say "heel." Give the leash a little more slack for the Afghan.

Forward.

Talk to them.

About turn.

Once around the ring.

Halt.

There are a couple of dogs who are very determined to lead. For those owners, what is needed is firmer handling. When your dog starts to go out in front of you, especially the ones that want to pull, use the snap-release or "snapl" on them. Also, when you do the about turn, give a snapl. *USE ONLY THE DEGREE OF PHYSICAL FORCE NECESSARY TO GET THEM TO HEEL PROPERLY.* Keep in mind, you are not trying to punish your dog, just signaling him.

This is just for the ones who have trouble with their dogs pulling.

Ready. . . . give the "heel" command *before* you step off. *No names.*

Forward.

Once around the ring.

About turn.

Use the snapl correction on the pullers. Slap your thigh to encourage them.

That's better.

Halt.

Let's relax for a minute or two. Does anyone have a question?

Carol - My dog wants to jump up on me as I'm walking him.
　　Should I do anything?
Trainer - No, not at this time. It's just playfulness and he will gradually work out of it. Be neutral to it. Respond with a "good boy" when he is walking properly.

For a persistent jumper I recommend to keep walking, sometimes even to speed up to a fast trot. This will keep him from jumping, since he can't do two things at the same time - heeling and jumping. Remember, know the sensitivity of your dog, and *only use the degree of force necessary* to induce the required change.

Now class, let me give you one of my "Psychological Edges" in training: **Timing**.

Timing is very helpful for competitive obedience trials and for dogs who are strong-willed. These are the pulling-leading dogs who manipulate and control their owners, initiating where to go, where to turn and how fast to walk. These dogs are telling us:

"I'll take *you* for a walk."

"Let's chase that motorcycle!"

"Hold on, we're gaining on that tomcat!"

It has been said that it's just as easy to learn a good habit as it is with a bad one. So let's condition our dogs' responses with **proper timing**.

Proper timing means always to give a verbal command *first* before you do any body movements. Pretend that your feet will not move until you say "heel." By developing proper timing you then become the originator and controller of your dog's movements and responses. This in turn creates positive behavior patterns.

So be aware of timing.

Now back to work.

Give the "heel" command before you step off.

Ready . . .

Oops, yes. The pick-up can and mop are right over there. We'll wait.

For those of you who might have forgotten the information at pre-registration time, I will go over it again.

1) Skip any morning feeding before class.
2) Do not give any water two hours before class. Of course, if it's hot and your dog needs water, give it to him.
3) Exercise him 10 minutes or so, before you come to class. For the more sensitive or excitable dogs I would suggest coming 10 or 15 minutes before class and using the outside sawdust ring. This way you will avoid accidents and needless distraction during class.

Ready class?

Be sure to say "heel" and watch your timing.

Forward.

For the dogs who are pulling, give them a snapl.

About turn.

Halt.

Forward.

Halt. I hear some names still being used. Remember, use just the "heel" command.

Forward.

About turn.

Halt.

I see most of you are giving a body signal for "heel." What's happening is, when I say "forward," you start leaning your body forward before you give the "heel" command. Your dog is capable of reading this body language. You want to be in charge of the "heel" command. This is very important. *THE HEEL EXERCISE IS THE CORNER BUILDING BLOCK TO ANY AND ALL FURTHER TRAINING.* You want to condition and develop fast, quick responses, which gives you more control over your dog.

So watch your **body signaling** and **timing**.

Ready.

Forward.

Talk to them. Keep their attention.

Here, let me handle your Shepherd for a minute.

Just stand in the center so that the class can keep moving. "Hi, boy! Whatcha doing? Look what I got for you, a goodie! Good boy."

About turn class.

"Oooops, let's go this way. Good boy. Here's another goodie. Boy o boy! How's that?"

Class, halt.

Do you see what I did with your dog? He is extra sensitive. I would suggest, when you work him for the first couple of days at home, give him encouragement and some tidbits as you are walking. Do not use the "heel" command until the third day. By then he will be used to walking on leash. He also shows some fear. Therefore, I would advise you to be extra gentle and patient with him. Eliminate any reprimands you might be used to giving him. Ignore the problem areas for awhile, if possible. He needs more confidence and trust.

Class, may I have your attention. Today and next week the sessions will be only 45 minutes long. The reason for this is, as I said earlier, we do not want to overwork our dogs, even in class. That is why I have several break/question periods. Generally, the newness for both owner and dog is somewhat taxing.

It is not how long but how well you do in training. 10 or 15 minutes of constructive handling is far superior for conditioning a happy, willing dog. One solid hour of training would be drudgery to the average dog. Remember "Plato" and the "Fly."

To serve and please his master is one of the dog's basic genetic behavior imprints. Practice these exercises daily. Do 5 or 10 minute sessions three or four times a day, if possible. Make the sessions short and sweet.

Be aware of your body telegraphing your "heel" command. When your dog reads this, he will be second-guessing you. This hinders your development of mastership. Use as little snap-release of his collar as possible. Instead, do more about turns. Left turns are also good for the pullers. When he is ahead of you and you turn left, he will bump in your left leg.

Wear soft shoes, sweaters or jackets for class work; no long coats or flaring dresses.

Before you go I'd like to tell you about a client and his dog named "Blitz." I think it will help some of you to understand the need for a change of attitude.

In the beginning of Blitz's training he had a no-one-has-ever-told-me-what-to-do-and-I'm-not-about-to-let-*you* attitude. He was very resistant to the daily workouts. Using physical force on such a strong-willed dog would only have made him more determined to resist the training. Since all living beings need love and attention, Blitz found out, (within three weeks) that the only way he could get any attention from me was to cooperate with the training. I reinforced his cooperation by praising him and with a tidbit. A few more weeks and he was working beautifully for me. He had those willing-to-please responses to my every command.

When the training sessions began with his owner, the old problems of resistance and defiance re-appeared. His owner could not get him to heel properly. Blitz seemed to have forgotten his training altogether. No more automatic sits. Yet when I took over, he heeled perfectly, did split second sits and went down on a hand signal only. So I drew this on the blackboard for the owner. . .

M.R.R. Grooves

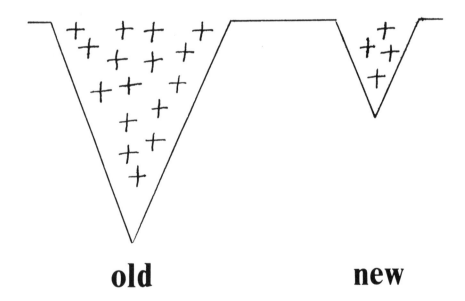

old   new

I explained to him that as long as he related to Blitz the way he did before the training, all Blitz could do was relate accordingly. It was a "**Memory-Relationship-Response**."

From all appearances, the owner agreed that his relationship with Blitz needed to be changed. But after a few more private sessions the owner finally confessed, "I don't want to be his master. Since he has been trained and knows all the commands, can't I just control him just with love and affection?"

I replied, "How could that be possible, when you cannot even get Blitz to heel without him pulling you?"

That evening, the owner made a decision. He wondered, if I would help him to find an new owner for Blitz. One that would be a master to him. I agreed.

After interviewing several potential owners, a young couple in their 20's came to see Blitz. I found that they too believed in the **master/owner** principle. Also, they understood that *catering does not develop control.*

I brought Blitz in the office to meet them. Just one sense-perceptive look and he trotted over to them and lay by their feet.

I asked both the man and his wife to work him in the training ring. Beautiful! He even worked *better* for them than for his former owner. More than likely, it was the beginning of a master-dog relationship, enhanced by early devotion, a combination that can't be beaten!

Select a quiet, secluded area to do your home exercises. You want to train with as little noise or distraction as possible.

See you next week.

SECOND WEEK

- Body Blocking

- Slow-Fast

- Stand-Leash Signal

- Pats & Strokes

- Arching

- No Name

- Missy

That's it. Heel your dogs into the training ring. Please check your dogs' collars. Make sure, they're on right for the proper snap-release effect. If you have any doubts ask, and I will check it for you.

With your dogs on the left side, we will be going counter-clockwise.

Ready . . . forward.

Watch your pulling dogs. Give the "snapl."

Be a little firmer with your correction, John.

About turn.

Halt.

For the dogs who are not pulling, give them some praise. Pet them a couple of times. "Good boy. Good girl." That's the way. Some of them are still a little apprehensive about all this newness.

You have a question, Joyce?

Joyce - Yes. Why shouldn't I praise my dog? I want him to like me, too.

Trainer - Thank you for asking a good question. If you praise a pulling-aggressive dog such as your Brandy, it's very possible that you encourage and reinforce his pulling. As for liking you, it would be better if he respected you and your commands as his master. Let him earn your praise.

Remember for the pulling dogs, when you do your training at home, it is much better to do an about turn instead of giving a snap-release on the collar.

Forward.

Watch your timing. Some of you are giving body signals. You need to condition *your* subconscious mind as well as your dogs to proper timing.

Halt.

Be more positive in your voice control. Don't ask your dog to heel - *tell* him. Use a normal tone of voice. A dog's hearing is approximately five times better than ours. So you need to express the commands with a firm tone, not a loud one.

Forward.

Do not restrain your dog, Jackie. Use a loose leash, and when he starts to lunge, give him a "snapl-heel" command.

About turn.

Halt.

Now is a good time to explain **body blocking**. This happens when your dog walks on an angle instead of walking parallel to you. You end up either stepping on his feet or getting tangled up with the leash. When you stop, his body is actually blocking you from walking forward. For some dogs, such as the herding breeds, this is instinctual. Some large breeds are also noted for using their bodies for blocking a man's movements. Now the last thing you would want to do is turn in the direction the dog is trying to *lead* you (such as to the right). If you do that, it makes *him* the originator of the heeling exercise, which puts him in control over you. This causes more work in training or more corrections than is necessary.

Walk 15 or 20 feet and turn a sharp left bumping into him with your leg. Say *nothing*. Let *him* figure out that, when walking on an angle, he will be in the way and will get bumped when you turn.

Do a series of left turns for 5 minutes. If he starts to heel wide, discontinue the left turns and do about or right turns. This will pull him back in. Another way to correct wide heeling is to walk close to the walls, allowing just enough room for him to heel properly.

Now for some new exercises: **Slow** and **Fast**.

With the "slow" command, reduce your pace to about half your normal walk. For the "fast," double your normal pace to a trot.

Here we go. Be sure to say "heel." Watch your timing.

Forward.

Loose leashes.
Slow.
Do not let them lead.
Normal walk.
Fast.

Joan, slow down a little. You're running.
Normal.
About turn.
Once more . . . about turn.
Halt.
Let's take a break for a couple of minutes. Does anyone have a question? Mmmm, I have your name on the tip of my tongue . . .

Rena - I'm Rena. My question is why the soft shoes and form fitting clothes? How do they help the training?

Trainer - Flaring coats and dresses add dimension to your body width, which makes your dog heel wide. Hard soles and heels are noisy when you walk. The dog does not have to watch your leg movements, he listens instead. This enables him to look around and be distracted. He does not give you his full attention, which is essential for training. The purpose of slow, normal, and fast exercises is to condition him to watch you closely and adjust to any pace change.

Any more questions?
Loose leashes, watch your timing and be sure to say "heel" each time you start. Ready . . .
Forward.
Fast.
Normal.
Slow.
Normal.
About turn.
Once around the ring.
Keep your eyes on your dog—your ears on me.
Don't let your dog lead. Correct him. When coming to the corners, slow down a little to signal to your dog that you are going to turn.
Halt.

Look around the class for a minute. Notice, how most of the dogs without prior training are standing. Let's make it easy on ourselves and our dogs. We'll teach them what they are already doing, the stand-stay.

To prevent the dog from becoming confused with the "sit" exercise, we will do a little foot work when the command is given. So as you are walking, I will give you the command, "Stand your dogs." You then give your dog the command "stand," at which time you slide the leash between the thumb and index finger of your left hand. Grip it at waist height and pull vertically 'till there is a strain on the collar.

Vertical Pull

Drift a step or two past the "heel" position and say "stay." This drifting past the "heel" position will make the "sit" exercise less confusing to the dog.

Ben - Could you demonstrate this?

Trainer - Sure. May I use your Doberman? Here's how it's done.

I will say, "Stand your dogs." Give your dog a "stand" command and, at the same time, a leash signal. Take a step or two beyond the "heel" position, after you've given the command and put a strain on the leash with your left hand. Then say, "stay."

a.

b.

Drifting

I'll do it again. If he starts to move, just pull up on the leash and repeat, "Stay, stay, stay." There, he did it. Here's your Doby. Thank you. Ready, watch your timing. Remember to say "heel," before stepping off.

Forward.

Slow.

Normal.

Be sure to pull up on the leash when you give the "stand" command.

Stand your dogs.

Take a few steps forward after the stand command is given, then say, "Stay."

Forward.

Halt.

For the dogs who are trying to sit, do not get into a physical hassle with them. Use your leg or foot to block their sitting. Let me demonstrate with Baron.

Leg Block

When you are about to give the stand command and the leash signal, angle your left leg so that your foot will be under the dog. In the case of Baron here, the leg will touch his rib and stomach area. If he still wants to sit, all you do is raise your left foot upward so it touches also his underside.

There, Baron's got it. Thank you Von.

Remember, you do not want to kick or force your dog with your foot. You just want a block effect by gently placing your foot underneath him. So it's more of a surprise response.

Forward.
Stand your dogs.
Forward.
Loose leashes.
About turn.
Don't forget the encouragement. Talk to them.
Slow.
Normal.
Stand your dogs.
Now keep the strain on the leash and repeat the "stay" command, then stand in front and face them. Good.

Keeping the leash up extend your left arm, so you can walk around your dog, and repeat, "Stay, stay, stay." Now go to their left, all the way around, and say, "Stay, stay, stay," for every stop you take. That's the way. Once more around and stop at the "heel" position. Now praise.

Forward.
Stand your dogs.
Go out in front and face them. Circle them slowly, saying, "Stay, stay, stay." Once more. Not too fast, take your time. Stop at the "heel" position.

Those whose dogs did not move, give verbal praise with two pats on the shoulder or chest area. "Good boy. Good girl."

Use pats rather than strokes. Pats are more related to a working comradeship. Remember the original purpose for all breeds is to have a working relationship with their masters.

I did notice that some dogs were moving as you went around them. A couple of dogs wouldn't let their owners get past the front of them. Instead of standing still, they turned with you making a circle within a circle.

Those "merry-go-rounders" will have to be handled differently. What they are expressing is fear. They are fearful of you getting behind them. This "Stay, stay, stay" command is a very good command for those of you who have a shy dog.

Let me demonstrate.

Charlotte, may I use your Annie?

Now watch. As Annie starts to move when I go to circle her, I stop. Then I go back out in front of her and over to my left (her right). As she starts to move, I pause. Then I go back to my right (her left). Each time, I arch further and further, until I make a complete circle around her. There, she did it. Thank you, Charlotte.

Remember, to say the command, "Stay, stay, stay" with every step you take and also to keep a firm restraint on the leash.

Ready, class . . .

Forward.

Slow. Some of you are still using their dog's name as part of the "heel" command.

Normal.

Fast.

Stand your dogs.

Each time, stand out front for this exercise.

Circle them.

Again. Walk slowly. Hurrying only keeps them tense. You want them to relax.

Once more.

Stop at the "heel" position.

Exercise finished. Praise.

Let's break in place. Any questions? No?

Well, our 45 minutes are about up. Practice the slow and fast heeling. Also the about turns along with the "heel" and "stand-stay" commands.

As your dog gets used to the "stand," use less and less physical restraint on the leash. Develop the "stand-stay" to where you can give just a slight pull up on the leash, along with the verbal command. Then ease the tension on the leash, and have them stay with a loose leash as you stand in front of them. Some of you might even get them to stand-stay on just the verbal command, without the leash signal.

See you next week.

Carol - May I ask a question before we leave?

Trainer - Sure. Shoot.

Carol - I have taken a basic obedience course before and was instructed to always use my dog's name first, pause, then give the "heel" command. Why do you stress not using the name?

Trainer - For several reasons. In most cases, when I give a "forward" command, the owner is concentrating on his movements. So, when the owner says the dog's name, he is already starting to move, which prompts the dog to move before the "heel" command is given. Thus, the name could mean different commands, such as: "Fido, heel. Fido, no. Fido, sit. Fido, stand. Fido, stay. Fido, come." This can become confusing to the dog. Each time an exercise is being taught, either the name command becomes one word to the dog, or there is a pause which slows down the responses to the command.

It is the first stimulus (the dog's name in this case) that has the greatest conditioning effect. Also, using your dog's name with *some* of the commands and not with others is inconsistent conditioning. Remember, they are creatures of habit. You want to condition them *properly*.

It's like two people sitting on a couch. You do not use the other person's name when talking to him. You only use the name, if his attention drifts, or if he leaves the room. When doing on-leash training, you should have the dog's attention because of the physical closeness. Encouraging your dog by slapping your thigh, along with your left and right turns, heeling slow, normal and fast, and doing about turns, conditions him to pay attention to you. So, there is no need to use the dog's name. After all, he is the only one on the other end of your leash.

Properly trained, your dog will always keep his eyes on you, waiting for the next command, so he can please you and receive your praise.

When doing your home exercises, you should always vary the distance you walk before you stop or make any turns. For instance, go 25 or 30 feet and do an about turn. Go 5 feet and stop. Change your speed. Normal, fast, slow. You do not want to mechanicalize your dog. *Do not overtrain.* 10 or 15 minute sessions three or four times throughout the day is fine. If your dog starts to tire out, cut the session short. You should quit while the dog has still the desire to please you.

Let me tell you about Missy, a three-year old Doberman bitch.

All she needed was one more leg to get an A.K.C.C.D.X. (C.D.X., by the way means "Companion Dog Excellent.") Mrs. K., the owner, had only one problem. Missy flunked the last six shows

in a row. She would go down on a long sit and not clear the high jump. Missy managed to have two major faults every time.

She was entered in the next show in Oakland. Mrs. K. had just two weeks to get her in shape. She called me on the phone and wondered, if I could help her. We set up an appointment for psychological testing for the following day.

Mrs. K. put Missy through her paces for me. I needed to see Missy perform in order to assess her weak points. Mrs. K. had been working her for a couple of months in a training class. The dog seemed bored with obedience worK. Even giving her a goodie didn't charge her up.

After carefully observing the dog in action, I recommended to Mrs. K. *not* to take Missy to Oakland. The high jump was not the problem. She was just plain overworked.

I advised Mrs. K. to skip all training for two weeks, then to do two or three sessions a day, no longer than 5 minutes each. Short and sweet. I suggested using tidbits when putting Missy through the exercises, and doing fast stops. Also, I recommended to change the sequence of the exercises, and to do only three or four "heel-halts," and then to quit. I asked her to contact me after two weeks for a private session.

What a difference! Missy responded like a rubber ball. As for her "problem" of the high jump, she sailed over the hurdle with 8 to 10 inches to spare. She was now ready to compete and was entered in the following show. I gave Mrs. K. last minute instructions to keep all sessions short, maximum 10 minutes, and to stop training three to four days before the show. For the morning of the show I suggested a 5 minute or so brush-up and, a few minutes before entering the ring, to do a couple of fast "heel-sits" with both verbal and physical praise in unison.

I received a call the Monday after the trial. Missy got her third leg, placing 4th with a score of 192 — the highest she had ever achieved in over two years of competitive trialing.

So, remember, it's not how long you work your dog but how well. Most dogs get overworked to the point of rebellion. Corrections and reprimands can be avoided by making the sessions short and sweet.

See you next week.

THIRD WEEK

- Sundays/Mondays

- Okay

- Sit

- Emotions

- Breaking Trot

- Stay

- Frankenstein

Good afternoon.

Before we start, I would like to mention something I saw happening in the parking lot. Some of you were letting their dogs lead, pulling you to your cars. This will weaken the training structure. Letting them pull you makes it more difficult to train them. It becomes a conflict. I call it **Sunday/Monday.**

People are used to working hard during the week and taking it easy on the weekends. But dogs can't read calendars and therefore, aren't capable of distinguishing a Sunday from a Monday. Whatever is permitted and accepted one day has to be permitted and accepted the next.

So be consistent. Have your dog heel properly to the car and also, when you are leaving the training ring. Heel in, and heel out.

Yes, John?

John - How do you let your dog know it's okay to sniff around and relieve himself?

Trainer - Thank you for asking. This would be a good time to teach the **release from control** command. You can use it after you're finished training him, at feeding time, or when walking him and he needs to go. If you see he is indicating a need to relieve himself while walking him on a "heel" command, give him some pats on the shoulder and say **"okay."** Encourage him to go out, away from the "heel" position. When he is finished, give a "heel" command and require him to return to the heel. For a quicker response, do an about turn rather than just keep walking in the same direction.

After a training session, give the **"okay,"** unsnap the leash, and he has his freedom. I will explain how to use this for feeding later.

Let's start training.

Ready . . . pat your left thigh when you step off with the "heel" command.

Forward.

Once around the ring. Loose leashes.

Now for the dogs who want to lead — give them a snap-release, when you do the about turn. For the other dogs, use the snap as little as possible. Just give a signal that lets them know you are turning around.

About turn.

Slow.

Normal.

Loose leashes. Some of you are restraining your dogs.

About turn.

Fast.

Normal.

Encourage the laggers. Here boy. Here girl. Pat your thigh.

Praise the heelers.

Correct the dogs that are leading.

Slow.

Normal.

Stand your dogs.

Stand in front of them.

Circle.

Once more. Stop at the "heel" position. Praise, if they deserve it. Let's take a question break.

Frank - Why the loose leash? What's wrong with restraining them?

Trainer - Training with a loose leash allows your dog enough leeway for your various turns. It also prepares him for off-leash training. Restraining the pullers and the aggressors encourages their strong will. Take notice next time you see a picture of an attack dog and his handler in action. A short restraining leash is used which the dog is pulling on. As a matter of fact, I use the restraining method to overcome the fear some duck dogs have with regards to water.

Frank - *A retriever who is afraid of water?* Never heard of one.

Trainer - It's happening all over, along with non-hunting hunting dogs who require special training.

Any more questions? Our next exercise is the "sit" command. We will give a different leash signal, so we don't confuse it with the "stand." It means pulling on the leash at a 45 degree angle to the rear of your dog. Remember, the leash signal for "stand" was straight up at a 90 degree angle from his neck.

May I use Blackie for a minute? Now I'll take my left hand off the leash and take a second grip with my right one, about 8 inches or so from the snap chain end. Of course, with the smaller dogs and toy breeds this length will be greater. I pivot in my waist to the left, pull the leash backward, bend my knees and, pushing down on his rump with my left hand, I say "sit."

Sit

I'll do it again.

Watch the timing.

I pull back on the leash, then give the command "sit" and push down on the rump. Once he is sitting, I repeat "Sit, sit, sit," tapping his rump each time. This pull-push works like the principle of a teeter-totter, putting him off balance and making the "sit" easier.

Thank you, Joan. Here's Blackie.

Let's practice. You can also stand alongside of your dog to get better leverage with the pull on the leash and the slight push on the rump. Be firm but don't be harsh—and have patience. Do it several times on your own, then we will do it on the group level. I will walk around to aid and assist anyone who needs it.

How're you doing, Von? Remember, we want to use only a minimum amount of force. It might be easier with your Great Dane and also with other dogs, who don't want to respond to the "sit," to convince them with a goodie. Hold a tidbit with your left hand directly in front of his nose and pull it simultaneously backwards together with the leash in your right hand. Don't forget to say "Sit, sit, sit."

Rena, your Dalmatian is wonderfully responding to this approach. He sits like a doormat. Once he sits on the verbal command alone don't forget to praise him.

Your Shepherd is very sensitive, Carol. Use less force. Be gentle.

Looking good, Jackie. Praise.

May I have your attention.

Each dog is an individual. Some are more sensitive than others. Some are eager to please and willing to learn. Others show resentment to your taking over. And after all, who can blame them? They have been in charge for long time and are now reluctant to let you take over and make them obey. Adjust your handling to the demeanor of your dog. Be gentle with the sensitive ones and firm with the strong-willed ones. Don't attempt a power struggle. Remember, *use only the degree of physical force necessary to accomplish an exercise.* Too hard or harsh handling can make your dogs non-responsive to training. They will refuse to learn or be so fearful that they will try to protect themselves by growling or snapping at you.

Watch your emotions when correcting. DO IT WITHOUT ANGER.

Let's do some work.

Forward.

Fast.

Normal.

Watch the corners. Don't let your dogs lead you around them. Correct them with a snapl-heel command.

About turn.

Halt.

Have them sit.

Be sure to give the command "sit" each time you stop.

Forward.

Halt. Sit.

Forward.

You can use the fast trot to perk up your dog.

Fast.

Remember, even when you speed up, they have still to remain at the "heel" position.

Once around the ring. Not too fast.

Breaking
Trot

Joyce, Mary, Frank, your dogs are breaking the trot. All three of you, drop back a few degrees in your speed 'till your dogs are not jumping when trotting. That's the way. Now increase your speed gradually, until you are up with the class again. Good.

What was happening here? When your dogs were running fast, through the excitement, their adrenals were charged up. We don't want to condition their adrenals but their mind. Only with a disciplined mind can our dogs control the lower levels of their behavior which are based on their survival instinct — their fear/aggression responses. We will explain these more in depth at a later time.

Normal.

Halt. Get them to sit. Give the command at the same time you stop. Watch your body language when you start off. Do not use the name when giving the "heel" or "sit" command.

Forward.

Mary, don't jerk your dog when she starts to lag.

Remember the **Fly** treatment. She is temperamental.

Get to know your dogs. Study their actions and reactions. Some are really con-artists. So beat them at their own game. Don't let them play or run freely before training sessions. Otherwise, they will be all played out. Put their energy to work in the training sessions.

Watch the corner tuggers.

Halt.

Stay

Hand

Signals

That's better. Now that you all have them sitting, we will teach them to stay.

Keep the leash in your right hand, put the palm of your left hand in front of their face and give the command "stay."

As you step off, watch them out of the corner of your eye. If they start to follow you, repeat the "stay" command and tap their nose with the palm of your left hand. Repeat, "Stay, stay, stay." Now step off and face them at the end of the leash. Some of you will want to circle them instead. Then stand out front and again say "stay." This time raise your left hand and show your palm to them. Now circle them.

Back to the "heel" position.

Exercise finished. Praise the willing ones.

Forward.

Fast.

Normal.

About turn.

Halt.

Give them a "stay" command, and with the leash in your hand, stand out front. Repeat the "stay" command. Return to them. Always go to their left (your right). That way you end up in the "heel" position without the need to pivot by their side. This could entice them to break the "stay."

Forward.

Halt.

Forward.

Halt.

Give a "stay" command and walk around them back to the "heel" position. Praise.

Forward.

Stand your dogs. For those who can do a loose leash stand, give the same "stay" signal, as we did for the "sit," and stand out front. For the others, only use the physical leash restraint as little as possible, when you circle your dogs. Repeat the command, "Stay, stay, stay."

Return to them.

Praise.

Forward.

Halt.

That ought to keep you all busy for the following week. Watch your body signals. Always give the "heel" command before stepping off. Practice slow, normal, and fast exercises. Do about turns and the "sit-stays." Use the hand signal for "stay" when doing the stand-stay exercise. Some of you can increase your home sessions to 20 minutes two or three times daily. Remember "Plato" and the "Fly." Have patience with your dog. Here is something to think about regarding next week's topic.

Dog owners are constantly phoning me for a magic word or solution to stop their dogs from nuisance barking, car and bicycle chasing, growling, snapping at strangers (sometimes even their owners), tearing up the house when left alone, whining, and jumping on the furniture.

They ask me, "What should I do? How should I punish him?" I always reply, "Re-establish your rightful position as his master. Do it with respect, and don't use the fear approach when you reprimand. When the dog recognizes your master-authority, only then approach the problem areas of his behavior. Otherwise, it's like a 6-year-old child trying to correct another 6-year-old."

Some owners do not understand how or why they permitted their dogs to take over and rule them. It generally takes place in the beginning, when a puppy is purchased. The puppy is chosen for its fluffy, cuddly, prettiness, its color, or because its ancestors came from Tibet. Sometimes, it's even chosen for a baby/child substitute. It requires and is given constant catering and, with a strong will-to-power, its demands become endless.

Yes, people have, in a sense, created their own **Frankenstein**. We will discuss this more next Saturday.

FOURTH WEEK

- Ringwise

- Dentist

- Master/Dog

- Equality

- Humanizing

- Mutual

- Make Haste Slowly

Good afternoon.

Very nice to see such changes already taking place.

Some dogs are even wagging their tails when they enter the training ring! In this profession this is sometimes called being "ring-wise." That is, a certain type of behavior is induced by a particular surrounding. This training ring could be considered a secondary reinforcement.

Now let's do some work.

Any questions first?

Susan - Yes. Please explain a little more about the secondary reinforcement.

Trainer - Sure. I'll use myself as an example.

During my teens I used to let the dentist fill the cavities in my teeth without using novocain. I had no fear. Later on, while in the Army, I needed some dental work done. I sat in the chair without any anesthetic. Bzzzzz—the drill started, and a second later went through my hollow tooth right into my jawbone. Out of the chair and out of the door I went. I was given orders to report the next day to have the dental work completed. I reported, but when the desk sergeant was not watching, I sneaked out. After my third getaway, the captain of the dental hospital gave me a direct order to stay. The dentist gave me five shots of novocain but I was still fearful.

Now, every time I walk into a dentist office and see the chair, I recall the memory of that painful experience and begin to perspire. That's what is known as secondary reinforcement or Memory-Relationship-Response.

So when you're doing these exercises here in the ring or at home, make sure that your dog's experience is pleasurable, not drudgery or fear.

Ready, class.

Loose leashes.

Do not lean with your body. Give the verbal command before you step off.

Praise, as you're walking, "Good boy. Good girl.

Forward.

About turn.

Halt.

Their sits should be automatically by now.

Forward.

Slow.

Normal.

Fast.

Normal.

Halt.

For those who are still using the leash signal for the "sit," be sure to pull it backwards. Otherwise, it can be confused with the vertical signal for "stand."

Sit

Leash

Signal

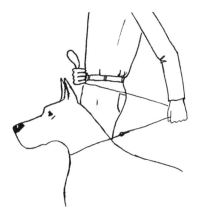

Forward.
  About turn.
  Correct the pullers.
  About turn.
  Stand your dogs.
  Be sure when you circle your dog to hold the leash up with your left hand.

Circle

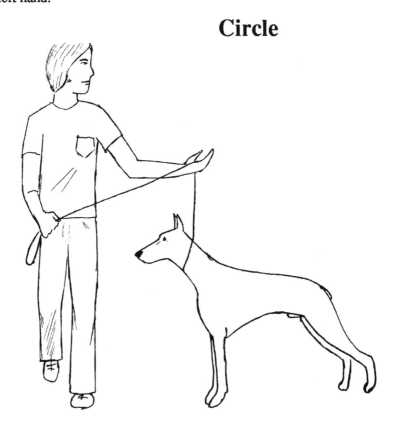

Circle them.
Again.
Go back in front of them.
Return.

Praise.
Forward.
Fast.
Trainer - Joyce, *slow down*, your dog's breaking trot.

Now, Joyce, you can start increasing your speed again. But as soon as he starts to break, slow down to where he is not jump-running.

Normal.
Halt.
Forward.
Give them a "stand stay."
Keep the leash in your hand and stand out in front of them. Good. Now circle them and repeat, "Stay, stay, stay," and go back out front.
Watch your dogs.
If they start to move, repeat the "stay" command.
Return to them.

Praise, if they earned it. Be real, be sincere. Good boy. Good girl, pat, pat. Once in awhile, you can give a goodie. Do it in unison — voice, touch, taste. Doing it this way is most effective.
Don't overpraise. Sometimes even skip it.

Will you please form on the other side of the training ring, where you all can see. I'd like to give a picturegraph-blackboard talk. The subject is on the three different relationships and how we relate to our dogs.

The first one is the **Master-Dog** Relationship.

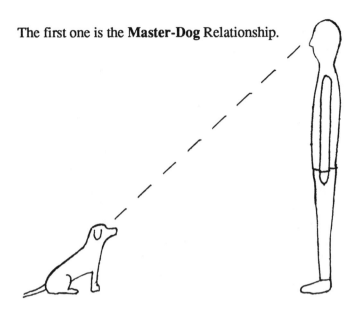

This is how mother nature intended it to be. The dog, being one of our domestic animals, has the genetic behavior imprint of servitude toward man—that is, to work for and please his owner.

Dogs have a psychological need to know where their territorial boundaries are. They rely upon their master/owner to define and establish both psychological boundaries in a behavioral sense and physical limits in a territorial sense (yard, house, room). When these boundaries are consistently established, dogs know what to expect when they stay in them, and what to expect when they cross them.

If the dog's master does not define boundaries, a dog is forced, like a wild animal, to form his own territorial boundaries and defend them with his teeth against all intruders, even human beings.

A *consistent* master-dog relationship gives our canine friend his security. Respect, not fear, is the foundation of these territorial limits.

Unfortunately, many humans practice a duality — a double standard. We say "yes," when we mean "no." We live in a world which requires us to read between the lines. Canine minds are of a single nature. They sense our innermost thoughts and feelings and cannot understand contradictions.

Let me tell you about a dog that could not cope with these double standards.

There was a couple who owned a 9-month-old dog who, for the past four months had been eating his feces. Clinically the problem was diagnosed as a dietary deficiency. Although supplements were given for it, the pup got progressively worse. What prompted them to call me was that the dog had begun to *sleep* in his feces.

It's true that puppies can develop the habit of eating their feces through playfulness, boredom, or from a dietary deficiency. But sleeping in its feces is a stage where the animal has lost all contact with his sense of cleanliness and self-preservation.

After six weeks of therapy training the dog avoided any physical contact with his feces.

When the clients came for a consultation visit, we found the cause. The wife was a disciplinarian, never permitting any real closeness between herself and the dog. The dog was not allowed in any part of the house except the kitchen where he had his bed. When the wife left the house, the husband (who was totally permissive) would encourage the dog to come in the living room and lay on the couch where he would pet him. Of course, this always left dog hairs. When the wife came home the dog was punished and put in his dog bed. This hot and cold treatment would blow anyone's mind. Being hyper-sensitive, the dog took the only way out — mental escape.

There was a happy ending though, for the couple agreed to establish a single standard of relating to their *new dog*. It never happened again that the dog ate or even stepped in his own feces.

The second one is the **Equality** Relationship.

In this one the dog is considered an equal member of the family with his own individual rights and expressions (which, in due time, he will let you know what they are).

Bordering on the edge of control, the dog is not much of a problem in puppyhood. Generally, when he is around 5 to 7 months old, he begins to fluctuate. At times he will listen to you, at other times he will not. As the puppy matures, he will less and less obey. It will get to the point where the dog is just too unmanageable to live with.

You see, dogs relate basically to people and other animals by the pecking order system. When a dog is not trained at all or trained with forceful-dominant methods and the owner does not permanently exercise the head position, then a strong-willed dog will be forced to take over by reason of his pecking order instinct. Should the owner want to re-establish his top position, the dog will challenge him.

Thus, the telephone callers ask me, "Why did my lovely dog snap at me, when I wanted to remove him from my bed?" Or, "For once I decided I wanted her off the couch. When I started to pick her up, she bit me. Now I'm afraid of her." These types of calls are endless.

79

The third relationship is the hardest one for our canine companions to adjust to—**Humanization.**

When used as a baby, child, boyfriend, girlfriend, mate substitute, or for something to adore, idolize, and worship, a puppy does not stand a chance. Neurosis is smothering him with a blanket of human emotions. The dog gets trapped in a kind of limbo world. He tries to perform on a human level (eating and sleeping with his owner) and does not have anymore the desire to perform as a dog (not wanting to breed or be bred). He just cannot relate to or identify with his own kind.

Like Don Quixote (*Man of La Mancha*), Fido is attempting to live an illusion. You will find with the 2nd and 3rd relationship, that the more you cater and bestow emotional love on the dog, the less control and respect you will receive from him. This is ironic but true. Catering does not develop control. Only psychological training and establishing mutual respect can.

From pure breeds to mutts, the basic imprint in a dog is all the same—devotion to please and serve his owner. This is our dogs' original destiny. For this reason they were bred.

An emotional relationship deprives a dog to live up to this purpose. It can even shorten his lifespan, since dogs are not genetically structured to fulfill the emotional needs/voids of their owners. Hence neurosis develops.

My experience is, that by emotionally conditioning and breeding such dogs, we can in a few generations create a new breed of dog— the born neurotic.

Ask the next dog owner whose breed is noted for working or protecting, "Why is he slinking and belly-walking?" Nine times out of ten the answer will be, "Beats me. I've never laid a hand on him or even raised my voice. He's been doing that since he was a pup."

I've had water retrievers that were fearful of water, requiring many hours of patient training to overcome it. Some retrievers even lacked the desire to retrieve. There are bird dogs disinterested in hunting — craving only the emotional physical contact with their owners. They demand the presence of their owners and can't be left alone even for a short time without acting up and showing abnormal behavior. Many male dogs owned by women are becoming over-possessive and over-protective.

Presently, 35,000 dogs on an average are put to sleep every day, and this number is increasing. Why are so many dogs being destroyed? These are not just strays but pure-breeds and family pets. In my opinion, the main reason in most cases is because of their **emotional** and/or **dominant conditioning**. The relationship between owner and dog got out of balance and subsequently out of control.

All the dog is trying to do is to fulfill the role we place him in. When we rewrite the script, the roles will change.

Now let's do some training.

Forward.

Loose leash.

Halt.

Give both verbal and hand signals for the "stay." Keep the leash in your right hand. Ready...leave them. We'll stand out and face them for two minutes.

Von, when you walk back to correct Baron, don't be so threatening, you're spooking him.

Return to your dogs.

81

Praise only those, who did not move.

Some of you are signaling when you step off. Watch your timing.

Forward.

Fast.

Normal.

Halt.

Forward.

Halt.

Forward.

Slow.

Normal.

About turn.

Stand your dogs.

Go out front. Keep the leash in your hands. I am going to walk by them. Watch closely. If per chance your dog starts to move say, "Stay, stay, stay." John, Dusty is moving around. Keep your eyes on him.

Return to the "heel" position. Praise, providing you know they are trying their best.

Forward.

Halt.

For those whose dogs moved at "stand-stay," put in more home practice. Have a member of the family or a friend help you with this. Give your dog a "stand-stay" and remain in the "heel" position. Let the person start about 10 feet in front of you and just walk around in a 10-foot circle. After a few times around have them make smaller and smaller circles until they are walking around 2 feet away.

Repeat this exercise with a "stand-stay" command. Remain with your dog at first. Later on stand out front and have the person circle your dog again. This is really a good practice for the whole class.

Jackie - Should I have the person touch my dog?

Trainer - Not now, since Laddie is a little man-shy at the moment. We will do that later. Also, the same advice goes for Carol and Von.

Let them gradually learn that there is nothing to be afraid of.

Forward.

Halt.

Forward.

Halt.

Once more. Forward.

Halt.

This is the method to practice at home for quicker sits. Walk 6 to 7 feet and stop fast. Do this several times in succession.

Forward.

About turn.

Fast.

Normal.

Halt.

They should all be sitting. Keep the leash in your hand, give them a "stay" and walk away. Stand out front and face them.

Good. Now walk around and back out front.

Return. Pause, then praise.

Remember, always be fair both in praise and correction. Control your emotions. Develop a balance. Make the praise proportional to the dog's response. A dog's respect and devotion can never be demanded, only earned by *mutual* respect and fairness. Above all, never trick your dog.

Forward.

Stand your dogs.

Return. No praise.

Forward.

Halt.

Good. Praise the automatic sitters.

Watch your body signals. Always give the verbal command before any physical motion. Use a loose leash.

The object is to have a fast responding, willing, working dog. Since you know how the relationship with your dog should be, you can now take control and become his master. This will make all of us happy — you, your dog, and me.

Spread out your daily sessions. If your dog doesn't respond as well as he normally does, cut the sessions short.

Use as little physical force as possible. You want to develop verbal control. Watch your leash signals. Be sure, you don't give a "stand" signal while wanting your dog to sit. Be easy on the sensitive, shy dogs. "Make haste slowly."

You want your dogs to reach their full potential in training. Therefore make sure, each level is solid before going on to the next one. Always review the previous exercises before teaching your dog any new commands.

Any questions?

Same time, same place, see you next week.

FIFTH WEEK

- Confused

- Crooked Sits

- Short Leash

- Repetition-Conditioning

- Mechanicalized

- Get In Touch

- Emotionally Dependent

May I have your attention. It's time to start the class.

I notice a few dogs standing. It's okay if you gave them the release command. Otherwise, they should be sitting.

Inconsistency is one of the major reasons why dog owners lack control, making it much harder to develop a master-dog relationship. Be consistent. Remember "Sunday/Monday."

Ready . . .here we go.
Forward.
Loose leashes.
Halt.
Frank, Mac is still leading you.
Forward.
Ben, you are jerking the leash when you step off. If you make this part of the command, it will make off-leash work harder. Give encouragement instead when you start.
Halt. Watch those "sits."
Joyce, I see you are still having trouble with Brandy's sits.

Joyce - Yes.
Trainer - I'll come over by you to catch what's happening.

Ready, class.
Forward.

Slow.
Normal.
Halt.

I see the problem. You are giving the "stand" leash signal. Brandy is somewhat confused.

Class, take a break in place while we work this out. Let me handle him for a few minutes.

There, he's doing the sits. Here, Joyce, do it several times to get him straightened out. That's more like it. Now for the rest of the time today, when you stop, just give him the "sit" command and be sure to pull the leash *backwards* with your left hand. If he doesn't want to sit, then push slightly on his rump or use the tidbit approach.

Back to work, class.
Forward.
Halt.
Forward.
Stand them. Circle and return to them.
Exercise finished. Praise.

Carol - What can I do when my dog sits crooked? His front is straight but the rump is on an angle behind me.

Trainer - Again, use as little physical force as possible. Manhandling him could cause resentment to the training. However, when you aren't firm *enough*, it's all fun and games to him. He thinks you are playing.

Here's what to do Carol. Let me demonstrate with Jerome.

As I come to a halt, I shift all my body weight on my left foot. This frees my right one. Now when I stop, I arch my right foot behind my left one and give Jerome's flank a tap.

Remember, class, the degree of the tap is dependent upon the sensitivity of the dog. I use just enough to get him to sit parallel to my side. Do this with a quick motion bringing the right foot back in place alongside the left one. Done properly, your dog will never catch on.

Be sure not to use the left foot to correct with. This would make the sensitive, shy dog afraid of your feet causing him to heel wide. Any more questions?

Forward.
Halt.
Leave them keeping the leash in your hand. Hey, quite a few of you forgot to say "stay" before you walked away.
Return to them.
Remember to us *verbal commands before movements*.
Forward.
Stand your dogs. Go out front and face them. I will come by and make contact with those who are ready.

Jackie, Ben, Carol, for you three it would be better to stand alongside of your dogs with a short leash held in the vertical position. They are not quite ready for a stranger's contact, so I will just walk close by this time.

Carol - Why the short leash?
Trainer - To prevent your dog from moving when I start to get close. Be alert. Catch your dog *before* he moves.
Back off a few more feet, Joan.
Go back to the "heel" position and praise, Susan.
Frank, put Mac back where he was. Now I'll come up again. Good.
Return to your dogs always passing to their left, back into the "heel" position.
Exercise finished. Praise the willing ones. Even give them a goodie.
Forward.
Halt.

Great. Most of the dogs sit automatically. This time, when I say, "Leave your dogs," drop the leash and walk away. Stop at 10 or 12 feet, turn around and face them. Some of you will need to keep your leashes in your hand, so just go out 5 or 5 ½ feet.

Ready . . .leave them.

No peeking over your shoulder, Charlotte. That indicates doubt.

Frank, that's far enough.

Some dogs can turn into you mentally, so as you do this exercise, you may want to give your dog a mental *"stay, stay, stay."*

Return to them.

Pick up the leash with your *right* hand. Now give two praise pats on the shoulder or chest area. "Good boy. Good girl." No praise for those who broke. Be sincere — not gushy.

You have a question, Mary?

Mary - Shouldn't I reprimand Sheba for breaking her sit?

Trainer - No. Just correct her by putting her back in place. Then repeat the exercise.

You do not want to reprimand until you know that they fully understand the command and are refusing to stay. Correction is repeating a command or position. A reprimand is a punishment for their not doing it.

Forward.

Halt.

This time be sure not to make dropping the leash part of the "stay" command. If you drop it first and give then the verbal and hand signal for "stay,", the leash would be the strongest part of the command. Why? Because it was the *first* stimulus. This will make off-leash training more troublesome. Remember, *the leash should not be any part of a command.* Just a neutral device.

Forward.

About turn.

Halt.

Leave them. *That's* more like it.

Return. Praise.

The next exercise is the "down" command.

With your dog sitting in the "heel" position, slide your left hand down the leash to about 4 to 6 inches from the snap. Bend your knees and pull the leash downward.

Down

Leash

Signal

At the same time, say the command "Down, down, down." Keep the left hand open until you touch the floor, then move it 3 or 4 inches up and down repeating the command "Down, down, down."

Let's do it.
Down your dogs.
Repeat the command several times, once they are down.
A few of you are struggling to get their dogs to go down. I will demonstrate how to overcome it.

Jackie, may I borrow Laddie? Here's how to do it.

Put a downward strain on the leash with your left hand as you squat down. At the same time, pull your dog's front feet forward with your right hand.

Repeat the "down" command several times. Thank you, Jackie, here's Laddie. He sure has a strong will.

Pull Feet Out

Let's practice.
Forward.
Halt.
Down your dogs.
Forward.
Halt.
Down your dogs.
Forward.
About turn.
Slow.
Normal.
Stand your dogs. Circle them and go back out front.
Return. Praise.
Forward.
Halt.
Down your dogs.
Let's have them *all* down. Some are still sitting.

Frank - I had Mac starting to catch on to downing. Now he's fighting it again. Why did you have us do the "stand" and "sit" exercises before we got the "down" message across? Wouldn't it have been better to just keep teaching the "down" command?

Trainer - *No*. Because if every time you stopped and downed your dog, you would be conditioning the "down" to be part of the automatic sit. (If this happens, cancel out the "down" exercises for a few days. Go back to them after your dog does not try to down automatically.)

Remember, repetition is the conditioning.

While we're talking about it, watch that you don't condition the praise as part of a command either. Do not praise over two or three times in succession. Skip it sometimes, even when your dog is working well.

Do not train your dog mechanically, especially those who are going to A.K.C. obedience trials. Beware of this. You don't want a mechanicalized robot performing a set pattern.

Fast.
Normal.
Halt.

93

Down your dogs.

Once you get your dogs down, give them a "stay" and walk away. With the leash still in your hand, stand and face them.

How are you doing, Joyce?

Joyce - Brandy keeps fighting it. He goes down only so far.

Trainer - That's what I call a "hard down." I see a couple of other dogs refusing to down also, but for different reasons.

Class, may I have your attention. Some of you are having a hassle in getting your dogs to down. Mainly, because of all the commands the "down" is the most submissive one. This is a defenseless position. In case of a shy, nervous, fearful dog, you really need to have a working rapport and mutual respect for one another. Thus they will have trust in you. Maybe I can illustrate this point by telling you what happened to me once.

When I first came to California in 1963, I was invited to the home of a countess from Denmark who was, at the time, living in Woodacre, outside of Fairfax.

We were conversing in the living room. I was sitting in a large over-stuffed chair; the kind you sink down into. This one was *extra* low to the ground.

The countess asked, if I wanted to see her dogs. I said, "sure" and started struggling to get out of the chair. She said, "No, sit there. Relax, I'll let them in."

She opened the glass doors to the veranda. In they came. One. . .two. . .three. . .four. . .I lost count as they converged on me. I just sat there as they all looked me over, sniffing me like a big bone. That helpless feeling of not being able to defend myself was overwhelming. Sitting in a chair barely 12 inches off the ground, I could see why the breed is called *Great Dane*!

Fortunately for me, they were all beautifully well-mannered. My apprehension in that submissive position was not justified.

Now, the strong willed dogs don't want to down—not because of fearr—but because they don't want to surrender their will to you. Like our friend Brandy here, who does not want to give up his throne/ruler position to his mistress. May I use Brandy to demonstrate?

When Brandy stops going down and is beyond the half way mark, I place my left foot on the leash and hold him in that position.

Hard Down

95

When you do this, be sure, he is close to the floor, so he can't return to the "sit" position. Now stand up and relax. Let him battle himself.

"Man (dog in this case) changed against his will is of the same opinion still." There is no greater defeat than self-defeat. Hassling this type of stubbornness only triggers them to fight back.

There, you see? Brandy went down.

Now I'll step off with a "heel" command, stop, and repeat the "down." Boy, you have a real strong one, Joyce! Just like his name. You should have started his training when he was a pup. Now he's down. You can take him now.

Rena - Why didn't you praise him when he finally went down?

Trainer - Brandy went down because he had no other choice. I praise *only* the willing-to-serve-and-please dog. (The will-to-serve and the will-to-power are fully explained in JELLY BEAN VS. . .) Why praise his defiance and resistance to your authority? Wait, until he tries to please.

Rena - But he *did* go down.

Trainer - Sure, only because his muscles gave in, not his mental attitude of acceptance.

Joyce - I have still problems with Brandy pulling me. It seems, the more I jerk, the more he jerks back.

Trainer - Being a hunting dog, your Irish Setter has a very strong will-to-power and a lot of energy. Pulling you is his outlet. What you can do is teach him to retrieve, preferably a tennis ball or something similar which can be thrown a good distance. In the meantime, you can stop his pulling habit by doing the **Airplane Propeller**. I'll demonstrate it.

Who will give me a problem puller besides Joyce?

Charlotte - Here's Annie. She pulls every once in awhile.

Trainer - Good. Yep, she still wants to tug. Here's how it's done.

With your right hand grip the leash further away from the loop end. This should give you a couple of feet dangling at your side. When you step off and she begins to lead, start the leash swirling by your right side, like an airplane propeller.

Then bring the prop out in front of you letting her walk into it.

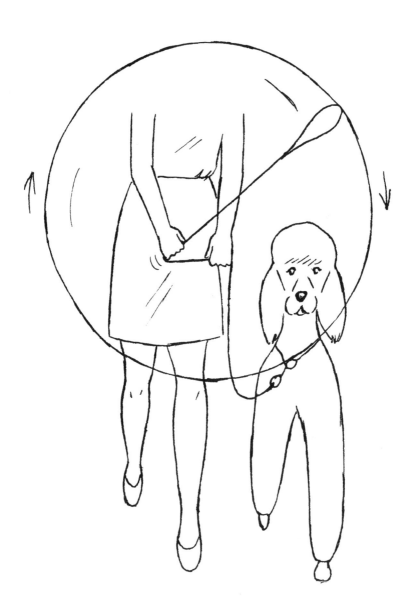

Airplane Propeller

Prop-side View

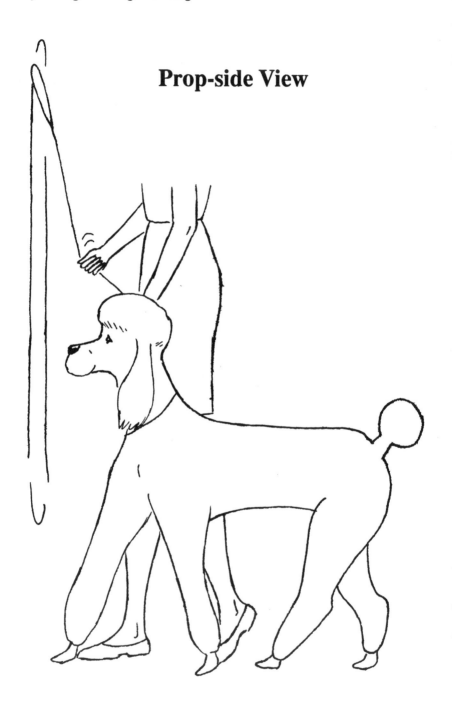

See, how Annie dropped back to the "heel" position?
I'll do it again.

You noticed, that after Annie backed off, I stopped the swirling and returned the loose end of the leash to my right side out of her sight. One more thing. This rotation is *always counter-clockwise,* so that the leash gets them on the tip of the nose if they advance too much. This is a dog's most sensitive area. The neck is the strongest part. That's why jerking some dogs (such as Brandy) is the hard way to go.

Joyce's 90 or so pounds are not enough to overcome 75 pounds of stubbornness. Dogs, having four legs, can exert more pulling power than a small woman with only two legs. Here, Charlotte, take Annie.

Let's practice. Ready. . .
Forward.
Watch your body signals. Some of you are still leaning.
Do the airplane propeller, John. Dusty's not responding to the snapl.
Remember to *stop swirling once they heel properly.*
Halt.
They all should be sitting.
Down them. Use the short leash on the hard heads. Don't praise Blackie! It took a battle to get him down. Praise only the willingness.
Forward.
Brandy's leading you, Joyce. Use the airplane propeller. That's the way. Don't be afraid that he gets his nose in the prop. He's smart enough to figure that one out fast.
About turn.
Stand your dogs.
Be sure to drift out a couple of feet beyond the "heel" position. Stand in front of them and I will walk by you. Don't let them move.
Good. Return. Most of them deserved some praise.
Forward.
About turn.
Halt.
Down your dogs.

Let's take a break in place. Any questions?

Joan - Earlier you told us not to stroke but pat our dogs.
Trainer - That's right.
Joan - Then it's wrong to stroke them?
Trainer - Not necessarily. Stroking can have a calming, soothing, therapeutic effect. It also can be done emotionally. The caressing can get pretty heavy. Dogs are often capable of tuning into our vibrations better than we can.

I'll tell you what. We will try it on ourselves. Give your dogs a "stay" command and drop the leash.

With one of your hands stroke and caress your shoulder. Get in touch with any feeling sensations. Now drop your hand, give it a shake or two. This time pat your shoulder. Get in touch again.

Is anyone not experiencing a different feeling between the two?

Susan - I'm not.
Trainer - Okay, relax. First, I will pat your shoulder. Now I'll stroke it.
Susan - Yes. . .I guess there really *is* a difference.
Trainer - Would you share it with the class?
Susan - The stroking had an intimate, emotional effect. The patting I conceived as friendly, as coming from a good buddy.
Trainer - Good. Thank you.

Joan - I guess I gave Blackie enough stroking for a hundred years. But I can't leave him alone for more than an hour or he wets or messes.

Once I left him for 3 ½ hours, and he almost destroyed my living room. He chewed on the furniture and tore up the divan. He messed in at least three different places. At that moment, I was ready to throw him out of the 4th story window.

When I go out for a dinner date, I hire a dog sitter. It's cheaper. I'm stuck, I guess.
Trainer - No, not really. Your dog is **emotionally dependent** upon human companionship. Blackie's background is similar to a 4 year old German Shepherd I de-humanized.

He could never be left alone for longer than 10 or 15 minutes. After that, the separation became so unbearable that he would start destroying anything in the room. In a few hours he would get so emotionally worked up that he'd have diarrhea. Imagine the mess *that* made.

So, like Blackie, this dog was never left alone. No local boarding kennel would have him more than once. Trying to find good sitters became such a hassle that the owners decided to do something about it. That's where I came in.

Since Blackie knows some commands, you can reprogram this dependency. Do the following: Anytime you greet him, give him only a couple of pats. If this still turns him on, then don't give him any.

While you are eating, reading, watching TV, or having company, give him a "down-stay" at least 10 to 15 feet away from you. This will help cut the cord of *emotional dependency.*

The separation, when you are at home, will help diminish the frustrational destructiveness, when you leave. Be indifferent to him, so he will not care if you come or go.

It probably started with you, so it will have to be ended by you. Once you have the behavior you want from him, give Blackie some affection. But only to the degree it does not encourage the *emotional dependency* to reappear.

That's about all, class.

PRACTICE EVERY DAY.

Short and sweet.

Be aware, of *how* you praise and relate.

See you next week.

SIXTH WEEK

- Half Eights

- Whiskey

- Boy

- Unison

- Cardinal Sin

- Before Reprimanding

- Houdini

Let's see. . . Good. I've counted twelve dogs. So that means, you're all here this time. Please don't miss any classes, if you can help it. These classes are progressive. Eliminating one rung on the ladder interrupts the steady climb to the top.

John, Von, the exercise for "down" was given last week. In fairness to the class, I'd prefer not to hold them up. Please, when we do the exercise, watch how it's done. Ready. . .

Forward.

Halt.

Forward.

Loose leashes.

Halt.

Forward.

Slow.

Correct the pullers with the "Airplane Prop."

Normal.

Stand your dogs.

Be sure to take a couple of steps beyond the "heel" position.

Face them.

Circle now back out front.

Return to the "heel" position. Remember to always return to your right counter-clockwise, so you end up in the "heel" position. Praise. Be sincere, no con-job. Your dog is capable of knowing the difference.

Forward.

Fast.

Normal.

Halt.

Von and John, give your dogs a "stay", then turn around and watch the person behind you.

Class, when you down your dogs use the beginning methods, so John and Von can observe how it's done.

Ready, class, down your dogs.

Ben, Joan, Frank, use the corrective method to get your dogs down. Von and John, watch how this is accomplished. You see how the leash is held short enough so they cannot return to a sit?

Ben - What do I do when I get Rommel's front part to go down only to have his back part go up? Just like he is now.

Trainer - Let him fight it alone. All you want to do is keep your foot on the leash. Stand up and ignore it.

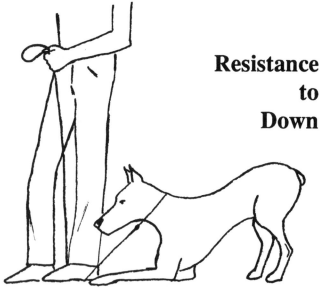

Resistance
to
Down

This is a beautiful opportunity to overcome his will-to-power and develop your master-dog relationship. It takes a lot of muscle straining on his part to maintain that off-balance position. Eventually, he will have to give in. *Do not praise.*

Let's work.
Forward.
Slow.
Normal.
About turn.
About turn.
Down your dogs.

John and Von, once you have them down, just stay in the "heel" position.

Class, leave your dogs. Be sure to give the "stay" command before you drop the leash and walk away. Ten feet is fine.

Keep your eyes on your dogs.

Correct them before they move with "Stay, stay, stay."

Once they get up, it will be necessary for you to return and repeat the "down-stay," then go back out in front.

Two minutes are up. Return to your dogs. If they broke the command, do not praise.

Now, we will do an exercise for walking your dog in public or in A.K.C. trials. It's called the **Figure Eight**. There are two purposes for this exercise:

(1) To teach your dog not to sniff or show any interest in another person.
(2) So they'll learn to stay close to your left side and not permit any object, such as a parking meter, tree, or person, to get in-between you and them.

This will be done gradually. In the beginning, we will do only half-figure eights using poles. The purpose for this is to get your dog used to the weaving. Up to now everything was done in a straight line.

This exercise is particularly good for developing your dogs' *attention span*, for when they aren't watching you, they will get wrapped around the pole. I find this exercise very effective for mentally retarded dogs. (Dogs that have kennelosis.) It sharpens their mental abilities.

Ben, you are about to pass the poles. So, instead of going around the training ring, do a left turn and start the class.

Half Figure 8

Ready. . .

Forward.

Encourage your dogs. Pat your thigh. Don't bunch up. Keep at least 10 feet behind the person in front of you. Otherwise, your dog might be distracted and get wrapped around a pole.

Halt.

We have a dog wrapped around the pole. Carol, encourage Jerome to come back around the pole to your side. That's it. Now when he is about to go the wrong way again, give a slight snapl and give the "heel" command.

Watch your timing. Give the verbal command, before you step off.

No body signals. Loose leashes.

Forward.

Keep your eyes on them. A little more "Fly" treatment, John. Dusty is starting to lag. He's somewhat temperamental. That's better.

Halt.

We'll just relax a minute , then we'll go once more around.

Forward.

Watch 'em. Signal, *before* they get tangled. Mary, more encouragement.

Halt.

For those who are by the poles, please return to the outside ring.

We will now do the full-figure-eight exercise. You will be starting about 5 or 6 feet back from the center lines of the poles. When I give you a "forward" command, say "heel" and go between them. Circle the other one making the figure eight.

When you go around the left pole, you will be doing an inside turn. If your dog gets in the way, give him a slight bump with the left side of your leg. (Use leash correction for the small breeds.)

For the right pole or outside turn give a slight leash snapl to have your dog keep up, along with some thigh patting and encouragement.

Any questions?

Full Figure 8

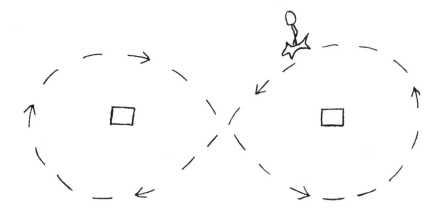

Joan - Which way should we turn first?

Trainer - It doesn't matter, left or right. In competitive obedience I start in the direction the dog does best in. So he's warmed up so-to-speak for the other turns. Most of the time, I will circle to the left first. (Unless the dog shows some interest to the post person on the left, just before the judge starts the exercise. Then I will circle the right post first.)

John, would you please position your dog at pole numbers 1 and 2 on my left. Susan, at numbers 4 and 5. Joyce, at numbers 7 and 8. Jackie, at numbers 10 and 11. I marked the starting spots with chalk.

The rest of the class on the sidelines, give your dogs a "down-stay." That way they can be relaxed until their turn.

Ready figure eighters.

Forward.

Bump them on the inside turns. Correct and encourage the outside ones.

Halt.

Forward.

Halt.

Thank you. Please return to the ring and down your dogs.

Frank, Joan, Rena, Ben, would you take the spot. Ready, loose leashes. Watch the timing.

Forward.

Turn left or right. Rena, watch Sir Galahad. He's wide on your outside turn. Give him a slight correction.

Halt.

Forward.

Encourage the laggers, praise the heelers, correct the pullers.

Halt.

Once more... Forward.

Do not slow up on your outside turns. That's the way.

Halt.

That's all. Please return to the outside ring and down your dogs. Von, Mary, Charlotte, Carol, please take the starting spot. Watch your dogs. Don't make the inside turns too tight. Ready...

Forward.
Halt.
Encourage your Afghan. Remember "Plato" and the "Fly."
Forward.

Charlotte, next time Annie gets tangled around the pole, have *her* come to *you* instead of you going around to her.

Halt.
Some of you are body-signaling your "heel" command. Remember, this makes the dog with a strong will-to-power the originator of his movements. So watch your timing.
Forward.
That's better. When training, you should do the thinking and your dog the following.
Halt.
The exercise is finished. Please return to the outer ring and down them. Let's break in place for awhile. I will tell you a story.

When I first came to California, I used to do a dog trick to entertain my ego, the tavern owners, and their customers.

The patrons would gather up three or four local dogs from the neighborhood, and I would take five minutes or so teaching them all how to "sit-stay." Then I'd line them up against a wall. The bet was that I succeeded to make them sit for two minutes. I was allowed two corrections per dog, but had to produce by the third try. If not, the drinks were on me.

Well, I found one neighborhood tavern in San Anselmo, where I was batting a thousand. The local dogs all seemed to be passive with low wills.

One day, Larry, the owner, decided it was time for him to win. I guess, he wanted to break even because the bet was for a week's lunches, double or nothing. Instead of using the local dogs, he wanted to use just one, his own eight-year-old Schnauzer. It seemed like a sure thing for Larry. The dog had eight years of conditioning and relating to him. Surely, he couldn't lose, when even his wife could not separate them at home.

Inside of five minutes, I had Whiskey staying glued to his seat with only one correction needed. It was a surprise to both of us. Larry still wanted to win. So he asked, if he could use a piece of meat to entice the dog. I said, "Sure, as long as we stand an equal distance away from Whiskey." Out came a slice of boiled ham. (Which I found out later, old Whiskey went bananas over. Even punishment couldn't break him from stealing a piece of it off the table at home.)

We started 10 feet away, ending at 4 feet. Larry and I stood side by side. He tempted Whiskey by waving the slice of ham, while I flashed my left hand saying "Stay, stay, stay."

Good old Whiskey did not move. Larry ended up eating the slice of ham, and myself eating a free lunch for a week.

There is a saying that what goes up must come down. Well, the day I came down was like being struck by a lightening bolt. It was such a shock to my ego that I have never put myself in that position since. I believe, there is always a remote possibility for lightening to strike twice in the same place.

"Boy" was the thunder bolt who taught me the real power of the "Eye."

I met Lester Bruhn at Dinucci's, a restaurant-tavern in Valley Ford. I was boasting, that if they had any dogs around, I would demonstrate for them.

Now the chances of finding any loose dogs in the neighborhood were slim because the total population of Valley Ford, at the time, was only 100 people. The next town of Bodega Bay was 10 miles away. Well, I lucked out, for when Les Bruhn heard about my bet, he offered to bring in his sheep dog (a Border Collie named "Boy") from his pickup.

I thought to myself, "Great! Maybe I can pick up a free meal with this dog." I had never seen a sheep dog up to that time. As a matter of fact, when I saw my first lamb with a long tail, I thought it was a freak. I was still a city hick from Cleveland.

I explained to Les the terms of the bet and he agreed, then brought the dog in.

When I took one look in Boy's eyes, I should have slowly walked away. I knew I was sunk, for I had never before or up to this time looked into the eyes of such a strong-willed dog. But a bet's a bet.

So I took Boy, who came along willingly, and put him in a corner, 25 feet away, and gave him a "sit-stay" command. I showed him my left palm and tapped him on the nose several times repeating, "Stay, stay, stay." He responded beautifully. I thought, "Hey, he's easy! I was just imagining his strong will. Now what kind of drink am I going to order?"

I walked confidently away and sat alongside of Les. I must have been grinning like a Cheshire cat. Les just smiled. Then I heard a snap of his fingers. ZING! Before I could flash a hand signal, Boy was at his master's feet.

ZING!

My mouth fell open wide enough to put both my feet in it. (Which I should have done earlier.)

One thing I can say for Lester Bruhn. He was a gentleman. He permitted me four extra tries to save face. I could have been given four hundred tries, but when Boy heard his master's signal, as far as he was concerned, I didn't exist.

After the house was set up, Les was kind enough to explain to me that sheep dogs use their eyes to "hold" the sheep and keep them from moving.

Let's do some more heeling. Watch your timing, loose leashes. Say "heel" then step off.

Forward.

Slow.

Normal.

About turn.

Halt.

Forward.

Halt.

Forward.

Halt.

All dogs should be doing automatic sits.

Remember, you want to gradually use less physical force as you develop verbal control. There must be *mutual respect in conditioning and reinforcing your dog's training.* Now be aware of how you start the next command. Do not make jerking the leash part of the "heel" command. Just put yourself in your dog's place. How would you react if every time you heard the word "heel" you were jerked by the neck? "Heel"—jerk, "heel"—jerk. I don't believe, anyone in this class would be overjoyed anytime the command "heel" was given. Isn't it better to say, "Heel - good boy," and give a tidbit?

Ready . . .

Forward.

About turn.

114

Stand your dogs. Go out front. Loose leash. We will have them stand for a few minutes.

Return, going to your right, back to the "heel" position. Praise. No strokes. Just matter-of-factly, "Good boy. Good girl."

Ben - I always understood that giving food during a training session was considered a cardinal sin, because the dog will not work unless he receives the tidbits.

Trainer - If you use it as a bribe, this is possible. But not when you use the tidbit reward properly - *in unison*. By unison I mean the verbal praise, the pats, then the goodies. Psychologically speaking, you condition his senses of hearing, touch and taste. Once these three sensations are instilled in the dog's subconscious mind, any time you use one of them the dog will relate to all three.

I have obedience dogs, field dogs and water retrievers come back for a refresher course, when some of the commands were not used for over a year. Yet in just one training session most dogs have total recall. The conditioned responses were there, just a little rusty. Pavlov proved that dogs can be conditioned to a certain response by ringing a bell before feeding them. Eventually, the dogs responded to the bell by drooling, even without the presence of food. (The Pavlov Principle is explained in JELLY BEAN VS. . .)

It is the repetition that conditions the unconscious mind.

Once you have conditioned the required responses (such as willingness, perkiness) in training, you can discontinue the tidbits, or just give them occasionally.

I have found this method highly effective on all dogs. It especially works wonders on the temperamental and the stubborn, strong-willed dogs.

When some experts say, "A dog will not work after the food reinforcement is stopped," then it should be equally true that a dog will not work after the jerking is stopped.

Again I have to ask, "What would you prefer, a jerk on the neck or a tasty morsel?"

Forward.
Halt.
Down your dogs.

Be aware, how you reinforce the "stay" command. Remember, the leash is *not* supposed to be part of the command. It's neutral. If you drop the leash first, that makes *it* the strongest part of the command. This weakens off-leash training. The dog reads this signal, and this makes him the originator. It puts him in control and can cause some problems, when you want to change your present relationship to the master/dog relationship.

Walk out about 15 feet into the center of the ring and face them. For those who are not yet ready for distant control, stay in the 6 to 8 foot "Gotcha Zone."

This exercise will be done for 3 minutes, and, like A.K.C. trials, will probably seem like three hours. Relax, but keep eye contact with your dog. If your dog begins to break, give a verbal, "no, stay" correction. Do not use body signals to threaten him. You want to develop your authority as a master with respect, not fear.

Von - Please explain about using the body in a threatening way.
Trainer - Leaning over, when giving verbal corrections, looks, to your dog, like a tree that is about to fall on him.

Body Threat

Frank - It appears to me that you have been avoiding saying anything about reprimanding. Why?

Trainer - Yes, I have, for several reasons:

(1) Using threatening gestures or reprimands in early training can create suppressed dogs. This applies especially to dogs who are temperamental. They work like a piece of wood, mechanically performing their exercises, without any spirited merriment. I prefer to train or show a happy working dog, who may lose a few points because of his eagerness, versus a perfect working dog with his head down and tail motionless.

(2) Most of the owners put their negative feelings, such as anger, into the reprimands threatening with both voice and body.

(3) Before reprimanding you should know:

   a. That your dog fully understands the command and had enough experience and practice in executing it.

   b. Your dog has heard you or seen your hand signal.

   c. Your dog is not overworked, which can create mental fatigue.

   d. You are not at fault. The dog is simply refusing to do it.

   e. The reprimand is necessary, and not just an outlet for your emotional anger.

In the eight week I will fully explain and demonstrate, how to reprimand without creating fear.

Ready, class? Let's wake up your dogs. You can step off with a "heel" command with your dogs in a "down" position.

Forward.
Fast.
Once around the ring. Watch them. If they start to break, give a snapl signal, slow down for a few feet, then return to the gaiting speed.
Normal.
Halt.

Great! I saw most of the dogs sat without any physical force. It's a good idea when practicing at home to say "sit," as you are stopping. Remember to skip the praise now and then. Once you have the conditioned response, give the tidbit occasionally.

Do the praise pats like a buddy.

Forward.

Watch your timing. Some of you are still stepping off first before you say "heel." Be consistent.

Slow.

Normal.

About turn.

Correct the pullers. Use the "Prop."

Halt.

Encourage the laggers. Hold their attention.

Sometimes I use a whistle, mostly the bobwhite call which is short and sharp. When the dog looks my way I say, "Good girl, have a goodie." Remember, you want your dog to watch you and your movements. This way you can condition split-second responses. Watch your dog. When you see he is paying more attention to the direction you are walking instead of focusing on your movements, do a halt, about or left turn. Do not let your dog's eyes wander around.

Another thing is sniffing. When training it is a distraction. Do not permit it. Get to know your dog. Be sure, you have his attention. Ready . . .

Forward.

About turn.

Stand your dogs.

Give the left hand signal at the same time you say "stay." Go out to the end of the leash and face your dog. I will walk by and make contact with your dog.

Repeat, "Stay, stay, stay," if they start to move at all.

Mary - Are they permitted to move their head?
Trainer - Sure.

Fine. Return to your dogs. Praise.

Forward.

Halt.

Down your dogs.

Forward.

Halt.

Most of you do not need to keep your left hand on the leash any longer. Just let your left arm relax along your side. Be sure you do not flash the palm as a signal for "stay." You can cross your forearm across your stomach if you wish. At a later date, when your dog does not need right-hand-leash leverage, you can hold the leash in your left hand for some heeling.

Forward.

Fast. Don't let them break trot.

Normal.

Slow.

Normal.

Joyce, don't hang the leash out in front of you. Keep it concealed along your right side, so it's not a threat to Brandy. You don't want to use fear as a controller. Let him decide, whether he wants to stay in the proper "heel" position or get his nose tapped. I will repeat the saying, "Man (Dog) changed against his will is of the same opinion still." Forcing him will only give you a temporary win. Soon, he will start pulling all over again. There is no greater defeat than self-defeat.

Rena - What you are saying is still not clear to me. Can you explain it a little bit more?

Trainer - Well, maybe the story of an English Pointer will help to make you understand what I mean.

It seems, "Houdini" had broken out of most every boarding kennel in Marin County. The owners had used up all the various methods of reprimanding to no avail, including the electronic collar and an electrically charged fence. They asked, if I could help.

When Harry H. arrived, I placed him in what I considered a secure run. I took a concealed hiding spot downwind from the run and watched. In less than ½ hour I found out, how he managed to break out of a cyclone-fence-covered run. He actually climbed up in the corner part of the run, hanging on with his feet like a monkey. Once he got to the top, he inched his nose, then his muzzle under the top of the fence.

When he got tired he dropped down, rested a couple of minutes then climbed back to the same spot and proceeded to stretch the fence 'till his neck was through. (Remember, this is the strongest part of a dog.) Then he used this leverage to pop the wires that were holding the fence in place. Out he came.

I caught him and locked him in the inside part of the run, then repaired the top.

We played this game for a week straight, locking him up at night or when I was busy training other dogs. Then the eighth day it happened.

Old Harry Houdini was just about half-way over the top, ready to jump out when he stopped.

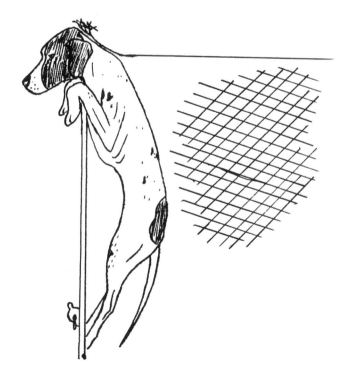

He appeared to be contemplating. Then he slid back into his run. I got over there real fast to give him some praise along with a couple of tidbits. The rest of the day he made no attempt to escape.

The next day I put him in an uncovered run. We watched him all day but he made no attempt to escape. Then I left him out overnight.

I don't know who got up first that next morning, me or the sun. But the sight that greeted me was sure beautiful; a glorious sunrise and Harry Houdini, still in his run.

I heard from the owners a year later. Harry had not attempted to jail-break since. Harry acknowledged defeat, which even some severe reprimands could not have accomplished.

Hey, I did it again. It's past 1:00 p.m.

Oh yes, one thing more. Next week and the eighth week will be 15 minutes longer. This compensates for the shorter ones earlier in the course. Also, It will give me more time to explain some important points.

Be sure to practice. Skip a day now and then. But don't skip coming next Saturday. See you.

SEVENTH WEEK

- Leave It

- Colonel

- Temperament

- Hard Sit

- Rocky

- E.S.P.

Good afternoon.

The parking lot picture is looking better every week. You all have come a long way.

Ready.

Forward.

About turn.

Stand your dogs.

Stand out front. Loose leashes. Circle them. Go back out front.

Return.

Exercise finished. Praise.

Watch your left and right turns. Some dogs know the ring and tend to speed up when you get to the corners.

Slow.

Normal.

Halt. Automatic sits.

Leave your dogs.

Go out 10 feet for a couple of minutes. Return. Exercise finished.

Have you noticed that some dogs started to go down, and one even went down, when you picked up the leashes? Does anyone know why?

I'll show you.

I have my dog on a sit-stay and I walk away. I return to him and with my left arm extended, palm flat, I bend down to pick up the

125

leash.

Ben - What you just demonstrated was a hand signal for down.

Trainer - Beautiful! That's it. Remember, dogs have not a complex, abstract mind but a single mind.

Always pick up the leash with your right hand. If you use your left hand, your dog could take it for a down signal. This creates confusion and conflict which results in your dog responding much slower to your commands.

Properly trained, the dogs should go down any time you give a left hand signal for it.

So, if the dogs go down (should you accidentally use your left hand to pick up the leash), you would give them a correction for *your* mistake—the hand signal.

Remember, inconsistency reduces the performance level, so watch your "Sundays/Mondays."

Now let's teach our dogs a command that is helpful, when you meet a loose dog while walking yours in public. It's called the "leave it" command, and it means just that - leave it, pay no attention. It takes two to tango, and in most situations, if your dog does not return the challenge, the aggressive dog will not approach to start a fight.

I will bring out a dog and tie him to the corner post. He will only have a few feet to travel. You will be walking around the ring in the usual pattern passing to the side of him. About 25 feet before you get to Ferdinand, give your dogs the command "leave it" and just keep walking. When your dog shows interest in Ferdinand, give him a snap-release and repeat, "leave it." Give another snap/"leave it" command and keep walking past. Repeat this anytime your dog starts to pay attention to Ferdinand.

Remember to use only the degree of physical force needed to get the correct response. Question?

Ben - Bill, Rommel has had a few fights. What if he should lunge at the dog?

Trainer - First and second time around give an extra firm snap. You do not want to get too heavy with the correction because he does not, for the moment, understand the command.

Generally, a few times around and most dogs know what is expected of them.

Ferdinand, by the way, is a lover, not a fighter. So he will not challenge your dog. Be right back...

Here he is. Everyone ready? Remember, if your dog stalls or shows interest, especially aggressiveness, repeat the command, and at the same time, back it up with a firmer snap-release. Keep walking past. The main thing is not to stop, even when correcting them. Watch your timing. Loose leashes.

Forward.

Keep your eyes on your dogs. Make them heel properly. Use the "Prop" for the pullers, encourage the laggers, praise the heelers.

Firmer with the snapl, Joan. Remember to say "leave it" at the same time. Do not praise, unless your dog is cooperating.

Praise, Susan, Cream Puff's already mastered the command. Pretty good for only two times around.

Halt.

Down your dogs. Give them a "stay," and we will take a break in place. Any questions?

Charlotte - What if Annie does not show any interest on her own? Should I still give the command?
Trainer - Yes. Along with praise.

Let's go back to work. This time we will walk past Ferdinand within his personal territorial range of 4 feet.

Ready. . .

Forward.

Give the command approximately 25 feet before the encounter. In some cases even at a greater distance, if your dog starts to show interest.

Much firmer, Joyce. Brandy's not paying any attention to you. Repeat the command, when you do the snapl, Jackie.

I see what you mean, Charlotte. One thing's for sure, Annie will never get in a fight, if she can help it. Von, easier on your leash snapl. Baron is sensitive and is showing some shyness. You don't

want him to be fearful, only uninterested. Much better, Joyce.
Halt.

I will bring Ferdinand up. And since your are all pros, I will bring
out a real Killer Diller. Give your dogs a down-stay. I'll be right
back.

Here's K.D. He is noted for his fighting record. He loves people
but not dogs. Now Killer is going to be lunging and barking at your
dog. The idea behind this exercise is that even though a dog
challenges yours (short of contact), your dog should not respond or
react to it. He should respond instead to the "leave it" command. Do
you have a question, Mary?

Mary - Can Killer Diller get loose?
Trainer - No, there is a double snap on his leash. Also, I will be close
enough to give any needed assistance.

Ready. . . Do not concentrate on this dog. In a way, pretend he
doesn't exist. Only be sure to give the "leave it" command and make
your dog do so. Carol, please start off for us. Stay about 10 feet
away from K.D. when you pass by him.

Forward.

Loose leashes. Some of you are signaling your fears by restraining. Your fear will only be transferred to your dog. True, there
might come a time when you will need their protection, but a
separate command can be used in that case.

Firmer next time you go by, Ben.

Praise, Frank.

Praise, Von.

That's a lot better, Carol. Do not praise yet. Wait, until Jerome
does not need a second command.

Joyce, let me handle Brandy this time around.

Keep walking, class. I'll be watching. Don't be concerned, if I
have to give Brandy a tap on his nose. From what I've seen, he's
almost immune to the snap-release and, when he lunges, the "Prop"
method should be more effective. Please stand in the middle of the
ring, so I can have Brandy's attention.

You see? Getting his nose with the leash backed him off. Let me take him around once more. That's better, Brandy, good boy.

Class, halt.

Here, Joyce, he has the idea now. With some more home practice he will get the hang of it.
Let's go around once more. This time, we will walk only 6 feet away from K.D.
Forward.

Correct only, if needed. You are all looking great. Even Killer Diller is quieting down. No one is playing his game.
Remember, class, the genetic imprint of our canine friend is to serve and please his master. What we are conditioning here is to interest our dogs more in pleasing us than getting involved in a fight.
Take a break for a few minutes while I put K.D. back. Down your dogs.

I use this same desensitizing method on dogs who are chicken killers.

John - I have heard, "Once a killer, always a killer." How do you change that?
Trainer - In the beginning of training I do not get involved with the dog's problem areas. I first develop a master-dog relationship, split second responses, mutual respect and trust.
Also, I never use physical force inducing fear when I reprimand. Once we have established communication, I then work on the problem area of killing chickens.

For instance, with a dog named Colonel I started off by putting a chicken in a 20 x 20 foot pen. Then I walked him inside and around the perimeter. When he showed interest, I gave him a "leave it" command and a leash signal. The next time around I repeated the command with a snapl. When he responded properly, I then gave (in unison) verbal praise, "good boy," then the touch—pat, pat, and a tidbit.

After a week or two of desensitizing him, I put in several chickens and left Colonel in the pen. I walked away in a direction that he was able to watch. I disappeared down the road, then sneaked back (downwind) behind some trees to watch him.

With no "stay" command he was permitted to walk around, which he did. One chicken must have been frightened, for it started running away from the dog. At the exact second he gave the running bird the "eye" and I bellowed out, "leave it!"

He spun around with a startled look as if to say, "Now where in the hell did *he* come from?!"

The final test came when I had my assistant hide behind some bushes with a chicken. I turned Colonel loose and let him romp in the field. Just as he was almost parallel with the bushes (which were downwind of him), my assistant tossed a cackling, wing-flapping rooster out.

Colonel casually ignored it. This time I bellowed, "Good boy!" His tail wagged as if to say, "Why, sure!"

Yes, you can remedy even the more serious problems.

Let's do some figure-eight work. This time, we will use people and their dogs for the posts.

Jackie, Mary, will you please be the posts for the first set? I've put chalk marks where you should stand facing each other. Susan, would you please take the starting point. Von, Joan, the next set of posts. Frank the spot. Ben and Charlotte the third set, Rena the spot. Carol and Joyce the last set, John take the spot.

Remember, handlers, when I say "forward" go in-between the two posts and turn either to your right or left. We have just finished teaching the dogs "leave it." So, if they pay any attention to the "posts," give them the "leave it" command.

Posts, you can also practice the "leave it." Your dogs should not be interested either.

Handlers, the first time around, stay 6 feet away from the posts; the second time around, 4 feet away; the third time, 2 or 3 feet away. You are desensitizing your dogs to the posts by gradually getting closer.

Remember, if they show any aggressiveness, be firm in both your snapl correction and your voice. *Tell* them to "leave it," don't ask them.

Are we ready? Do not have a too loose leash, Von, Just about 2 to 3 inches for this exercise. Be sure you give the "heel" command before you step off. Keep your eyes on your dog. The posts will take care of theirs.

Forward.

Make a large circle first time around.

Halt.

Posts, some of your dogs were too interested. Watch them.

Forward.

Halt.

Do not make a smaller circle if your dog is acting up.

Halt.

Once more. . .

Forward.

Around 2 or 3 feet this time. Frank, use your knee on the inside turns.

Halt.

Please exchange places with the post nearest you. Ready. . .

Forward. Large circle.

Mary, Sheba is lagging. Give her some encouragement. Joyce, Brandy's doing it again. Instead of giving him a snap-release just get the "Airplane Prop" going. This will teach him to heel properly. You have to demonstrate that you are his master and he is not yours. That's the way.

Halt.

This time do the 2 to 3 foot circle.

Forward.

Watch them closely. Correct the pullers. Say "leave it," if they're too interested.

Halt.

Thank you. Please exchange with the person who has not done it yet.

Ready, handlers? For you it should be easier.

Charlotte - How's that?
Trainer - Your dogs are used to the others by now. They're desensitized.

> Forward.
> Carol, Jerome's lagging. Give him a goodie. See how it works?
> Halt. Closer this time.
> Forward.
> Halt.
> Again. Last time.
> Forward.
> Remember to praise, when they are heeling properly.
> Halt.

Exercise finished. Thank you. Will you all please return to the outside ring. Let's relax for some minutes. Down your dogs, give a "stay" and drop the leash. I'd like to do some blackboard talk.

Dogs are like snow flakes. No two are exactly the same. This is the reason, why you can never find the carbon copy of that perfect once-in-a-lifetime dog you owned before.

The word **temperament** has many meanings in the dog world. Maybe I can explain, so we can better understand it.

Temperament

I consider the word itself to mean the even balanced expression of the dog's (or human's) mental and emotional makeup. For instance, a dog who has a good temperament will relate to other dogs, animals, people, places, and things without expressing fear or hostility. One that accepts his master's training or even a properly executed reprimand without showing fear, shyness, resentment, or defiance.

The dog with a balanced temperament is the one who accepts the veterinarian's handling (inoculations, etc.) without expressing either introverted or extroverted behavior. He manifests just a middle course of action and reaction.

Now from this center point of a balanced temperament, a dog can go either to the left or to the right. First, I will explain the left side.

TEMPERAMENT

Temper. (The Extrovert)

This can be described as being exasperated by a trifling circumstance, to manifest bad feelings by action, to give way to anger.

This type of dog will let you know what he feels about anything right here and now.

Just like a toy poodle that was in my last class. When I had the owner start walking around the training ring for the first time, little Kan just flat out refused to go. I was informed that this was the way he behaved at home. When walked, he'd plant his four feet firmly on the floor, and with all of his six pounds he would say, "Make me!" Of course, if the owner would have tried to drag his little dog, this would probably have resulted in a trip to the vet.

I had the owner walk slowly for 10 or 15 feet ignoring Kan. Then, when he stopped, he talked to the dog, "Hey, whatcha doing away back there?" He knelt down while talking. When Kan came up to him, he was given a couple of pats and praises. Then the owner stood and said, "Well, let's get going," and he merely started walking. No jerking or tugging. Finally, Kan started walking with him which he was then praised for. It worked, to the surprise of Kan's owner.

In the past, there was no way Kan would walk, and the owner always ended up carrying him.

A dog that expresses temper will let you know how he feels in a physical way.

TEMPERAMENTAL

Mental. (Pertaining to the mind.)

Now, here's the con-artist. The other side of the negative coin. Like Kan, this type of dog also dislikes training. But instead of expressing his dislikes outwardly, he does it inwardly.

There are some noted working breeds today that are no longer willing to be worked or trained. We have a few here in the class. They express their displeasure by being temperamental. If you do not handle them with kid gloves constantly, they will sulk. Actually pout.

I have seen them in the show ring. Their facial expression is dishpan. They'll sometimes throw a rear leg out like it was disjointed and even go swayback in conformation. If you use any verbal or physical correction, they will look like you've beaten them. What actors! If they were on stage, they'd win an academy award.

Dogs of this type need to be studied for their various patterns, acts, and reactions. In their subtle ways, they are great manipulators to get out of doing what the owners want them to do.

The roles need to be reversed. The dog should respond to the owner rather than the owner respond to the dog.

Like the book, *Games People Play*, we need to beat them at their own mental games Because of past experiences we know what their responses will be to certain commands.

I will use Tom and his 2½ year old Golden Retriever, Mabel, as a good example.

Tom had previously attended a class here. In the training ring Mabel would heel one or two feet behind Tom. When the "fast" command was given, Tom would slowly increase his trot figuring Mabel would catch up to him. It never happened. When he gave a correctional snapl, she would come up for a few seconds then drop back even further. She would do what I call the "hard sit." (Sitting with her rear end 2 or 3 inches off the floor.) And she'd hold it. That only proved to me that she was not weak by any means.

Tom's greatest desire was to enter A.K.C. obedience trials. He had been to several other basic obedience classes and was always told to praise constantly.

Now, the first thing I told Tom, was not to use the dog's name along with the command. Next, to stop all praise. I advised him not to use the chain collar but to use a show leash instead. I told him to be particularly aware of his body language and timing.

At first, Tom questioned the reason for stopping all praise. I asked him, "Has it been working for you?" Of course, he had to say "no." I suggested, "Then you need a new approach."

The more small changes took place, the easier it would become for the biggest one, to de-throne Mabel. Tom needed to stop responding to her. I instructed him, not to jerk or pull the leash when she was lagging, and not to look back. Also, when he stopped, not to look at her directly, just to watch her out of the corner of his eyes. To work her 5 minutes, twice a day. The remaining time she was to spend in her run. She should not receive any attention from him, except when he trained her.

I think, that all this was harder on Tom than it was on Mabel, but it paid off. Within one week with her home activities drastically reduced, Mabel was only 6 inches off when heeling in both normal and fast paces.

In the following week, Mabel was really radiant. She was now heeling perfectly. More beautiful yet was her tail wagging merrily through all the exercises—even the stand-stay. What an actress. Only now she loved the part.

Tom said, it was the first time in 18 months of training that she showed any desire to be worked or to please him. It had always been the other way round.

Now he could enter her in A.K.C. obedience after all. Before, he had been told by others she wouldn't show.

I told Tom that now was the time to praise the willingness. I reminded him to do it sincere, short, and sweet.

As you can see, by getting to know your dog, you will then be able to use the right approach to training.

Carol - Tom's story was encouraging. Only I don't really understand, why Mabel reversed roles and became a willing worker. I've had prior class experience too, and you described my Jerome to a "T." Could you explain?

Trainer - Sure. A temperamental dog like Mabel indicates a sensitive base nature. The slightest trifling experience exasperated her and she subtly expressed it.

You can compare it to a house plant sitting in your kitchen window. Notice how its leaves face the outside. By doing this, the plant receives its needs from the sun. Now rotate the plant, so the leaves are no longer facing outward. What happens?

Carol - They turn themselves around to face the sun.

Trainer - Right. The plant's needs were momentarily denied, so it changed to fill them again. Well, Tom did exactly the same thing by not giving her any praise (which she'd been getting whether she worked or not). *She* had to change, in order to receive it again.

Every living being needs love and attention. Give the attention to your dog for the behavior that you *want*. Reinforce the positive behavior and slowly but surely the negative behavior will begin to fade away.

To sum up the three different expressions, I will use this illustration. Suppose a person is driving down the road and a car pulls out in front of him. The even-**temperament**-driver would slow down but not react to the situation.

The **temper**-driver would feel indignant and honk the horn angrily.

The **temperamental** driver would brood all the way home and then subtly take it out on the family.

Frank - Hey, Bill, would you elaborate on how the negative behavior slowly fades away? How can this work on a biting dog?

Trainer - The trick is that you do not reinforce the aggressiveness, only the friendliness or neutral behavior.

Frank - For example?

Trainer - Well, about five years ago, I almost met my match.

Rocky was his name. He was the first - and until today - the only dog that I could not take from the owner and put in the run. The owner sure didn't exaggerate when he told me about Rocky's aggressive, unpredictable possessiveness regarding the family.

With the owner and his family living in San Francisco it was necessary, to walk Rocky in the early morning hours on a deserted street. If anyone got within 10 feet of the owner, all 100 pounds of

German Shepherd would lunge out to the end of the leash growling protectively.

No one outside the immediate family was permitted in the house unless Rocky was locked in a far room. Of course, this just frustrated and aggravated Rocky more toward strangers. *They* were the cause of him being separated from his family. Also, for every house visitor there was a door to be replaced, having been shredded by Rocky.

This was the dog, who was challenging me in my own territory. Normally, when a dog enters a strange area, he shrinks his aggressive will down. Usually, he will not challenge a dog or person in their own territory. This is one of the reasons, why I require the dogs to come to my territorial ground, rather than entering and challenging them on theirs.

Well, Rocky had no respect for this territorial code. So I had the owner put him in the run.

For the next three days, every time I came close to the run, Rocky would charge the gate. The 10 gage fencing was showing the effects of his chewing, and he eventually was able to get his muzzle through.

There was no way I could get to him to snap on a leash for training. So I tried a new approach. Desensitizing. Every time he'd start to charge, I would turn my back and walk away. I did this for a couple of days and Rocky stopped charging. He just stood and watched me pass by.

Then I began to toss in a piece of liverwurst when I passed him. The first few times all he did was watch me. Yet when I returned later, the liverwurst would be gone.

We played this cat and mouse game for a few more days. Finally it happened. Rocky got hooked on liverwurst. He actually wagged his tail when he saw me coming. I was then able to enter his run and take him out.

The reprogramming was slow but sure. His behavior became puppyish and playful. Of course, his owners needed training too, since they had permitted Rocky to rule them for over three years.

Let's do some more exercise. Ready. . .

Forward.
Slow.
Normal.
Slow.
Normal.
About turn.
Watch the corners. Some dogs are taking them ahead of time. Do not let them anticipate. That permits them to take over.

Fast.
Normal.
Halt.
Down your dogs.
Leave them.
Return to them. No praise yet. Just stand in the "heel" position. Now pick up the leash with the right hand, which should be neutral. Do not let them anticipate. They are still under the "down-stay" command. Correct them, if they get up.
Now praise. "Good boy. Good girl."

Joan - What if Blackie gets up after the praise? Is it okay?
Trainer - That depends upon what level of performance you want from Blackie. You can use praise as a release command. Only it might possibly slow down his overall responses.

Von - How's that?
Trainer - Let's take heeling for example. While you are working them, they are being praised for their effort and willingness, yet they are Èrequired to heel and be under control. It's only for their cooperation.
    Do you see the two different responses they would be conditioned to give? Remember, "Sunday/Monday."

Ben - How do we release them from the down?
Trainer - The same way you release them on the leash. Give the praise, then say "okay." For instance, "Good Baron, okay."

    While we are on the subject of a release command, in the third week I mentioned using the "okay"-release word for feeding. This eliminates the barking, running around, the jumping up on you spilling the food. It is also a reminder of their training.

Give your dog a "sit-stay" command facing you. Place the foot dish in front of him and wait a few seconds or so. Then give the release command "okay."

The first couple of times they might tend to hold back. So give the "okay" again along with some pats. If they break, reinforce the "sit-stay" by giving a couple of slight taps on their nose with your left hand repeating, "Stay, stay, stay" each time.

Once you have conditioned this part of the feeding routine, *always be sure to release them to eat.* The reason I stress this is, because some dogs are so conditioned to obedience that they will not eat unless you give them the "okay."

Frank - You mean to say when you walk away the dog still will not eat?
Trainer - Yep, some won't. That happened with Eric, a German Shepherd from Sebastopol.

Eric had just gone home with this owner, Claudine, after going through eight weeks of private training. The last session with both the client and Eric went smoothly. He responded and worked for her perfectly. As they drove out of the kennel driveway, I couldn't help thinking that this was one dog who wouldn't try to revert after his training. His total cooperation and willingness to please her was beautiful.

Later that evening while in the middle of dinner, my bubble burst. Claudine was on the phone and urgently wanted to speak with me. I left the table wondering what could have gone wrong.

I asked her what command she was having problems with. "None," she said. "Only Eric won't eat his favorite food. He just sits there staring and drooling."

Oh boy, did *I* goof! I forgot to tell her about the "sit-stay" and "okay" for feeding! Eric had been sitting over 15 minutes and would not break. (Even though she did not tell him to sit or stay.) Once Claudine gave him the "okay," he ate heartily.

Ben - How do you determine that a dog is conditioned?
Trainer - When the dog gives the same performance level and responses

for seven days in a row. For the average dog you might have a couple weeks of yo-yoing before they become leveled off.

Ben - Then you train five days a week with a two-day break.

Trainer - That depends on the individual dog and where he is coming from, as they say today. Some dogs need a break in the daily training. Preferably train for three days, break one day, then train for three more days. Skipping a day now and then is fine. With some strong-willed dogs it is necessary to work them seven days a week.

Now let's get to the **recall** exercise. First, once around the ring to wake them up.

Forward.

Fast.

Keep going.

Halt.

For the recall you will be giving your dogs a "sit-stay" command. Holding the leash in your right hand step out in front and face them. Watch your timing. Say the verbal command first, then use the hand signal. They should all be sitting.

Ready. . .

Leave them.

Now you will say your dog's name, give the command "come," at which time you move backward quickly. As he catches up to you, stop and at the same time give the "sit" command. Praise, when he does it.

Rena - Hey, I thought we weren't supposed to use our dog's name when giving a command.

Trainer - You are using the name in this instance to get his attention, because your dog is no longer physically close to you. If you already have his attention, then you will only need to say "come. "For home obedience I also use two sharp hand claps, which are a stronger command than the verbal one. The name can also be used for the dog's personal identity. For instance, when a certain dog is doing nuisance barking, I will use the name first. So I can direct the verbal command to that dog only. Or, if I have several retrievers on a "sit-stay" command, I use the name identity. Thus, I can give one a retrieve command "fetch," and the others will stay put, while the dog whose name I used makes the retrieve.

Now back to the recall. Remember to use as little physical snap on the leash as possible. The object is to have your dog come in fast and willingly, not because you physically towed him in to you.

Let's do it. Leave your dogs.

Call your dogs.

Now practice for a few minutes on your own. I will walk around to give any needed help.

Rena - Why do they have to sit? If it's for home obedience, couldn't they just stand, as long as they come?

Trainer - I prefer them to sit for two reasons:

(1) They are now doing automatic sits when working with you. This reinforces them.

(2) Your dog is under better control and more relaxed when sitting.

Return to your dogs. "Heel" position.

We will now do individual recalls. While I'm working with one person watch, so you can learn by this experience. Down all your dogs, except John.

John, step off with a "heel" command, take a few steps and stop. Leave Dusty. Call him. Have him sit. Finished. Praise. Give him a "stay," return to the "heel" position and down him.

Carol, ready? Leave Jerome. Call him. Don't jerk the leash. Just hold it and run backwards. Good. Praise.

Ready, Frank? Call Mac. He's moving too slow. What you want to do in home practice is to run backwards faster. This will entice him to come quicker. Also, give him a tidbit before you leave him and after he comes and sits. Return to the "heel" and down him.

Von, Baron does not seem to be performing today, as he normally does.

Von - Well, I did work him a little over an hour just before class.

Trainer - I'd say that's the reason.

Let's skip Baron's recall. He's had it.

Mary, leave your dog. Don't call him yet, wait. Sheba was ahead of you in anticipation of it. Now she's fully sitting. Call her. Fine. Praise. She's a nice working dog now. Keep up the good work.

Next. Call 'em. Thank you.

Next. Be sure to always give the "stay" command before you leave your dog, Joyce. This is what is making it difficult for you to change your relationship with "Hard Head Brandy." When you call him, do not run backward. It only charges him up. For you I suggest just to stand still, when you call him. Be sure that he sits. Call him. Good. Thank you.

You're next, Ben. Leave Rommel. Call him. Ben, you need to watch your timing. You stepped off, before you gave the "stay" command and Rommel started to follow you. When you did give the command, he went back to the "sit."

It's the *inconsistency* that conditions a good worker into a poor one with slow, hesitant responses. Rommel wants to work for you. Only he gets somewhat confused by the mishandling. Be consistent.

Rena, leave Sir Galahad. Now call him. Praise. You're both doing great.

Next. Give more praise, Frank. Thank you.

Okay, Joan. Call your dog. Be sure to always have him sit.

Next. Thank you.

Take a few steps more, Susan. Leave your dog. Wait. She's ready to fly. Now call her. Boy, Cream Puff sure does have wings. One way to stop her from running into you is to give a "sit" command ahead of time. This way, she will be sitting out in front of you instead of on top of you. You don't want to lessen her quickness. Also, if she attempts to run past you, use either your right leg or left one according to which side she is about to pass. This creates a funneling effect centering her in front of you.

142

Left   **Right**

We are finished. Any questions?

Frank - Yes. I've been waiting for the chance. I hear, you use the word "nein" instead of "no." How come?

Trainer - Oh boy, I guess, I'm also conditioned. Yes, I use it for private training. I don't teach it in a group classes, because some people are adverse to using a German command. I use "nein" for a verbal reprimand because it has a much sharper sound to it. "No's" vibrations are lower, weaker sounding, and it does not carry as far for distant reprimands. I even use "nein" when I train a dog in Cantonese. It is a double-edge command.

For instance, when I leave a dog with a "down-stay" and he starts to get up, I will give a "nein." This stops his movement and he returns to the "down."

Ben - Can it be that he is going down as a submissive gesture?

Trainer - Possible. Only it also works for the "sit-stay." When he begins to stand up, I give a verbal "nein" reprimand. He stops getting up and goes back to a "sit-stay." It is very effective in stopping hunting dogs from chasing rabbits, or dogs from barking. Some of my clients even use it for their children!

Now, if the dog got up, then I would give him several "neins," take him back to the exact spot, then repeat the command.

Frank - Bill, I have one more question. Do the dogs know the spot where they were supposed to be when you return to them?

Trainer - Yes. Some dogs know exactly where their home property boundary lines are, even though they aren't marked with bushes or a fence.

When returning the dogs to the spot where they broke, I purposely put them further back than they originally were. This penalizes them in a sense, like in a football game. Some dogs will even try to go down at the original spot as we pass by it. Remember, they have an acute sense perception. They know where they were laying by certain temperature changes on the ground that can be registered by them, along with their own body scent. This all helps them to zero in on the spot.

I use this sense ability to correct dogs who will during a "stand-stay" move a foot or two when you aren't looking.

Examination. Here's how it's done.

I give the dog a "stand-stay," preferably on a cement floor which is cool. I position him so that the body weight is equally distributed. Then there is no excuse for moving. I draw a circle around each foot with chalk, allowing ½ inch or so beyond the perimeter of the foot. Then I turn and pretend I'm interested in a picture on the wall. Now this is the part that really gets him.

When I see the dog moved a foot, I put it back in the circle and at the same time give him the verbal "nein, nein, nein." Then I repeat the "stay" and look away.

After he did not move for 5 or 10 seconds, I increase the time to 30 seconds. Then to a minute. Then to 2 to 3 minutes. I find, this takes a little more time than the snapping of his collar and correcting him. But the chalk-circle method does not create displeasure to the command itself.

Any more questions?

Practice your exercises daily. Make them short and sweet. It's not how long you train but how well. Make every minute count. Concentrate on what you are doing. Be aware of your body signals. Develop your timing. Get split-second sits. Correct only when necessary. This does *not* mean reprimand. Praise their efforts and willingness. Encourage them, do not force them. Anytime they do a hard sit or a hard down, let them fight and defeat themselves.

Develop their attention span by talking to them. Praise the worker, correct the puller with the "Airplane Prop," encourage the lagger.

Use as little physical force or snapl as is necessary for the moment. You want teamwork, comradeship, and companionship based on mutual respect, not fear of a reprimand. Be consistent in your handling.

If you are pressed for time, or you don't want to train that day, it is much better to skip it. Your dog is very capable of sensing your frame of mind.

Joyce - Bill, you're kidding.

Trainer - Nope. I've had some clients that were able to turn their backs to their dog, give a mental "come" command, and the dog came to them. I've given a mental "Good boy. Good girl" to certain dogs, and every time they responded by wagging their tails. Of course, I know this is far from scientific proof. There is a possibility that I was giving some kind of signal unknowingly. But there is one type of experience though that makes me believe our canine friends have E.S.P. It is, when a client takes an extended vacation without any set date in mind as far as returning. The pick-up week and date are left open. Quite a few dogs will act up between 48 to 72 hours before I am informed of the owners' arrival. Sometimes it's a phone call or a post card stating the date. This happened even with some dogs that were left for months at a time.

Now back to your homework. After the fourth or fifth day, begin doing the recall on a 25 foot long 1/8 inch thick nylon cord. Use it the same way you are using the leash. Only now you will be recalling them at a distance of 10 to 12 feet. Once they have mastered this range, increase it to 18 feet, then to the full 25 feet. *Do not do off-leash recalls yet.* You want to always have the physical back-up if necessary in the early part of training. If some strong-willed dogs find out they can get away from you, it will take double if not triple the time and energy to overcome it. It seems, a negative habit is more easily mastered by a dog than a positive one. The only reason, I would assume, is because the positive habit requires a discipline, where the negative one does not.

"Make haste slowly." Have patience, patience, patience... then more patience. Dogs are creatures of habit. So let's condition and reinforce only the positive, good habits.

Next week will be our last group session.

John - Bill, can I use a rope instead of the 1/8 inch nylon?

Trainer - I would not advise it. Some dogs are able to distinguish it not only visually, but also by the weight of it hanging from their collar.

Frank - Speaking of negative habits, is there any way I can stop Mac from breaking his chain when I put him outside?

Trainer - I would not advise keeping a dog on a chain. Fighting and pulling on it only strengthens his will-to-power (neck area). It seems paradoxical, but chained dogs usually become more aggressive and hostile. I would suggest building a run for him.

See you next week.

EIGHTH WEEK

- Nickels

- Stubbornness

- Baroness

- Subconscious

- Conformation

- Right Foot

- Watch

VIII

Good afternoon. I see everyone's here,

I wish I could fully express the "Before and After" picture I see in this class. It always amazes me how the beautiful transformations take place in a short period of less than two months. Your dogs are both peaceful and happy in having the territorial boundaries of their behavior established. Many of you also appear much more relaxed and confident in your master-dog-control relationship. This is the meaningful part of my work. It's a reward that is lasting.

Let's get to work. Be aware of your body language. Be sure to give verbal commands before any physical movements.

Forward
Fast.
Normal.
About turn.
About turn.
Halt.
Forward.
Slow.
Normal.
Fast.
Halt.

Great! Several dogs are sitting on a dime and giving a nickels change.

Down your dogs. Let's break for a couple of minutes.

John - Bill, I read in a book where it said that a negative characteristic of hunting dogs is their stubbornness. They have to be forced to respond in obedience training. Can you comment?

Trainer - I sure will! Like a hungry dog that someone just tossed a juicy bone to.

Breeders for centuries have strived through selective breeding to maintain this "stubbornness" in their hunting dogs. It is a much *needed* trait. Good hunting dogs must overcome the forces of Mother Nature.

For example, the large mountain lion dogs need it to pursue the cat over mountainous terrain. The Coonhound needs this stubbornness to tree its quarry. The Beagle needs the stubborn determination to overcome the resistant force of the briar patch. How else could they root the cottontail rabbit from its protective shelter?

Weimaraners, Pointers, Springers, and English Setters need this trait to be able to hunt all day long through high weeds. (Especially when their owners are poor shots.)

The Labrador Retrievers need stubbornness to force their way through thick tules that even a hunter cannot penetrate. The Chesapeake Bay Retriever needs it to overcome the swift currents and icy temperatures of the river. Otherwise, how would his master get that fallen duck or goose?

Yes, they all need this desirable characteristic trait which I call strong will and determination to endure and overcome obstacles.

Using the force method in their training only triggers their will-to-power to resist! The dog owner/trainer must understand this mechanism and train without force.

As far as obedience training a stubborn hunting dog is concerned, let me tell you about a German Shorthair Pointer's accomplishments in obedience.

Her name was Baroness. When I purchased this $25.00 runt-of-the-litter pup, I never dreamed she would end up teaching me a thing or two.

At the early age of 14 months, she finished her C.D. (Companion Dog) degree within 13 days with 196+ point average in the first three shows.

C.W. Meisterfeld   **Baroness**   **Milo Pearsall**
Oak Park, Michigan   **November 10, 1957**

She was given the "Will Judy Award for Canine Distinction" (Album of Great Dogs of the Past and Present, 17th Day of December 1957) for this accomplishment.

I can still recall the third show held by the Southern Michigan Obedience Training Club, Oak Park, Michigan, November 10, 1957.

At high noon, a team of handlers and their dogs put on an exhibition. What a beautiful sight to watch the flawless performance. The participants consisted mostly of the natural working German Shepherd Dogs. Just one look, and you would know what breed would, more than likely, take most of the first four winning placements in the obedience rings.

I did not believe the sporting dogs were considered competition, because when I went to get my arm band I was informed by an official, that "The sporting breeds are shown in the next ring."

I replied, "Yes, sir."

"This is an obedience ring," he said.

Again I replied, "Yes, sir."

His comment then was, "Well, you have a German Shorthair Pointer, take her to that ring for conformation. *This* is for obedience."

I said, "Yes, sir. Her name is Baroness Meisterfeld, and we are here for the obedience trial."

Now with such a large entry it's possible, he didn't remember a Shorthair in the line-up. Afterwards, when we went to pick up the various trophies and awards, it was quite obvious what breed was considered for the first place. "German Shepherd" was already written on the cash award envelope. So they had to cross out "Shepherd" and write in "Shorthair."

Mr. Milo Pearsall, a noted trainer and authority on working dogs, was our judge that day. It was one I will never forget.

Baroness had a very stubborn strong-willed determination, which she expressed by winning placements in A.K.C. field trials along with state water retrieving trials. Then in 1962, she won the National Retriever Championship for that year. I guess, she didn't want any other dog to beat her. Thus, she did what could be considered in any point system trial "the impossible." She earned a perfect score of 500 points.

The judges claimed, they never would have believed a dog could be handled and controlled to such perfection. Coming from retrieving trial experts, this was a compliment.

The 1963 trial was not held that year for reasons unknown to me.

In Ohio in 1964 she took the National German Shorthair Pointer Retriever Championship again. Her first place in the National German Pointing Breeds Retriever Championship was the frosting on the cake.

Hey, who started me rattling on about my Shorthair?! Let's do some exercises. I've put your dogs to sleep. Ready. . .

Forward.

Fast. Let's wake them up. Once around the ring.

Normal.

Stand your dogs.

I will come by and stroke their top line. Don't let them move, when I come by.

Mary, watch your dog. Sheba's doing some subtle moving when you look away.

Jerome's showing some shyness. Have a friend practice with you Carol.

Return to your dogs.

Exercise finished. Praise the willing ones.

Forward.

Fast.

Around once more — it's a good way to lose weight.

Normal.

Halt.

Forward.

Halt. Correct the poor sitters.

Forward.

Halt.

Some of you are still signaling your "heel" command. Watch your body language.

Down your dogs, give them a "stay" and take a break in place while I explain how to reprimand your dogs.

In the early part of training reprimands should not be used when your dogs goof. If you do, it generally will turn them off to future training. Thus, their true performance potential will be hampered. Remember the words of Plato, "Early learning should be pleasurable."

You have been up to now teaching your dogs through daily repetition what is required of them. Also, you taught them what you expect by giving verbal, hand, and leash signals.

It takes time for all this to get registered in their subconscious memory bank. Just like learning how to drive. You practice, practice, practice. One day, while you're driving, a car in front of you comes to a sudden stop. This causes you to stop also. You then realize, you did not consciously think to stop, it was automatic. Your practicing paid off. The subconscious mind is now conditioned.It is the same in training your dog. Think, how much more difficult it would be for you to learn to drive, if the driving instructor yelled at you all the time. Here is a very important key to reprimanding your dogs without them becoming fearful.

REPRIMAND ONLY WHEN YOU ARE POSITIVE, THE DOG IS DEFYING YOUR COMMAND. Be sure, he perfectly understood what you wanted from him, before you do it.

Most training books and instructions recommend to always scold the dog, to let him know you are angry. This is gaining control through inducing fear. The dog becomes fearful of his handler and of being reprimanded.

The key to reprimanding is *NOT TO USE THE EMOTION OF ANGER—BUT TO DO IT AS A MATTER OF FACT.*I'll show you what I mean. I will walk hurriedly right up to Jackie. Now, Jackie, what did you feel?

Jackie - Apprehension!

Trainer - Okay, let's say, I also hit you. This then would reinforce your apprehension to my approach. Now, the next time I approach you the same way, what would you do?

Jackie - I would run away or probably strike out at you when you come close.

Trainer - Right. When I reached the Gotcha Zone (or before), you would need to take a course of action, flight or fight.

Now, Carol, I will approach you again. What were your feelings or reactions?

Carol - No change, I didn't feel apprehensive.

Trainer - Why?

Carol - Because you were casual. You didn't look threatening or angry.

Trainer - That's it. Good for you.

Remember class, the survival instinct is in all of us. The sensitivity of a dog determines when that instinct will be triggered. So, when you go to your dog, walk normally. Remain cool, calm, and collected.

Do what has to be done without emotional anger. Then your dog will not develop a fearful nature.

Fear control is only good for the Gotcha Zone, up to 6 to 8 feet. The dogs, who know all the commands and perform only well when on leash, know they're outside of the physical fear zone of a reprimand, when they are off-leash.

Fear itself is a mental projection of a happening. So do not project a reprimand to your dog. Do it matter-of-factly. Short and sweet. Be fair. Always be sure (as with praise), he deserves it. *AND WHEN IN DOUBT, DON'T!*

Joyce - Do we also give a snap-release when we say "no?"

Trainer - Yes. Generally, the snapl should be done very lightly, since it is just a chain signal. Be firmer when using the snapl for a reprimand. I would say, do it at least two or three times firmer than the very light snap-release correction. This way, your dog will be able to distinguish the difference between leash correction and leash reprimand.

Again, do not use the emotion of anger. You want to maintain the respect level of your dog, not tear it down. Do the physical and verbal reprimand in unison. "Nein," snap. "Nein," snap. The physical part enhances and reinforces the verbal one. As you progress in training, the physical part of the reprimand is not used — the verbal reprimand is sufficient.

Of course, if your dog does not accept the verbal reprimand, then it will be necessary to back it up by giving a physical reprimand along with the second verbal one.

Remember, that once your dog understands the commands and the right responses are instilled, but he is clearly defying you, do not repeat any command without physically reinforcing it.

However, the object when teaching your dog any exercise progressively is to cease using the lower level of training (which is the physical) but have your dog respond to your verbal commands or hand signals. You want to develop your mastership and authority with respect on the first command.

If after working your dog on leash he suddenly becomes aggressive, more than likely this indicates that the dog is being mishandled. The handler is at fault — not the dog.

Now, if your dog becomes aggressive toward you when training or reprimanding, the first thing you should ask yourself is "why?" Is it possible you used the emotion of anger and over-reprimanded? Remember, if a dog gets fearful, it's either flight or fight. Physically restraining the dog with the leash forces him to become aggressive toward you. Even a mouse will fight, if it feels cornered with no way out.

Ben - Bill, aren't we supposed to praise right after we reprimand?

Trainer - No. Suppose you goof up a job and your boss approaches you and slaps your face. Then he immediately pats you on the shoulder and praises you. What would be your reaction?

Ben - I don't know if I would be fearful because of the slap or exuberant because of the praise. I guess, I'd be just plain confused.

Trainer - Right. So let a reprimand be a reprimand, a correction be a correction, and praise be praise.

Let's get back to work.

Forward.

About turn.

About turn.

Halt.

Remember, when practicing do not mechanicalize your training. You want your dog to respond to commands - not a set training pattern.

Leave them with a "stay." Again, watch your timing. It's stay, hand signal, then drop the leash.

Keep walking all the way around the ring. For the dogs who are still breaking, hold the leash and stand out front. Do not walk too close to the other dogs.

Return to the "heel" position. Pick up the leash with the right hand. Praise. Remember, the right hand is neutral. The left is the command hand.

If you pick up the leash with the left hand, it would be taken for a signal to down. If you're not aware of this and the dog goes down, he would then get a reprimand for being so sharp. This slows a dog's quick responses to the hand signals.

Forward.

Halt.

Forward.

About turn.

Halt.

Down your dogs.

Leave them. Be sure to give a "stay" command. Once around. Stop at the "heel" position. Pick up the leash — *do not let your dog get up.*

Now without repeating the "stay," drop the leash and walk away. Your dogs should not move as they are still under the "stay" command.

Joyce, Susan, Joan, Ben, return to your dogs and give a couple of reprimands without emotional anger, just matter-of-factly. Now repeat the "down-stay" and walk away.

Joyce, I suggest that you stay with Brandy.

Pick up your leashes. They are still to remain down.

Exercise finished. Now, give praise along with the "okay." Release, if you wish. Ready...

Forward.

Halt.

Down your dogs. Give them a "stay" command. I will do some more black-board talk. Please make sure you can all see.

Have you ever been in a large group of people, and in the crowd a certain person stands out from all the rest? The person seems to have such a strong personality. Upon meeting the person face to face you see the reason. The eyes are strong and steady. You think, "No one would be able to rule this person." It is a strong-willed individual.

This is the same will-to-power some dogs have been expressing in the class. These are the ones that pull when the owners want them to heel properly. They're the hard sitters and the hard downers. They fight every exercise not wanting to give in. Yet, when I worked some of these dogs, they responded to my commands because they sensed I meant business. I won't permit their will-to-power to rule me. This is why a few of you are still working at establishing a master-dog relationship. Be consistent, persistent and determined to control their will-to-power.

From their genetic origin dogs are pack animals with a ranking order, where someone has to be in charge. Thus, you have to become your dog's master and earn his respect to control him.

Charlotte - I have heard that, if you train a dog when he is too young, he will rebel when he gets older. The books say that this is the juvenile stage of rebellion toward the authority and that you cannot prevent it.

Trainer - This will not happen when you train a strong-willed puppy properly. Remember to use only the degree of physical force necessary, when training. You want the respect of your dog. Thus, he will obey you, regardless of his strong will-to-power later in life.

Progress slowly and patiently. If you use a fear-reprimand with a strong-willed dog, it's only a matter of time before he rebels.

It's like the story of the little girl who was told to sit down. After telling her that for the tenth time, the exasperated mother picked the little girl up and forced her to sit in the chair. Then the mother said triumphantly, "There, you're sitting now!" Her daughter replied, "Yeah, but I'm standing up inside!"

Now that basic attitude and the force method is what will make a dog rebel to his early training upon reaching maturity.

Dogs communicate this strong will to each other. For instance, two dogs are walking down the street. Their eyes meet for the first time. They stare at each other. Hackles rise, tails go up. They are communicating, challenging each other. They are finding out who is top dog. Who is going to be the ruler, who the subservient subject. It is a "battle of wills." This is and eye to eye combat.

If one of them drops or turns his head, this is a submissive signal. The war is over and the victor does not need to start any physical action. The loser walks away with his tail down symbolizing defeat.

Now when two equally strong-willed dogs meet and neither backs off, it is necessary to decide by fighting who is top dog.

The "leave it" command can be very helpful when walking your dog in public and you meet one of these dogs.

Ben - Bill I have a stumper for you. Why is it at dog shows, even though the conformation dogs aren't considered obedience trained, the handlers still have no problem in showing their dogs?

Trainer -Actually, the dogs are trained. No dog can be shown or judged if he is not obedient to the handler's conformation requirements.

Next time you are at a show, watch how a handler shows a dog. They are either holding the dog's head with their hand or by a show leash, thereby controlling the dog's will-to-power through the neck area.

Have you ever seen two dogs romping? One will roll over and let the other one playfully chew on his throat. What the dog is doing is submitting his will-to-power over to the playmate. It's symbolic to the dog.

Groomers are conditioning the will-to-power of small breeds when grooming them. They use a grooming table that has a short leash hanging from a rod which holds the dog in place by his neck.

(Once so conditioned, the drop cord is unnecessary.) Dogs handled this way are conditioned to have good manners.

Show dogs and hunting dogs are transported to their destination in show crates. Dogs are also crated at grooming shops.

The crate shrinks down the territorial boundaries of the dog's will-to-power. This enhances the handler's and groomer's ability to control strong-willed dogs.

Yes, conformation handlers are also trainers of a dog's will-to-power, but in a different way. Yet the result is the same - a well-mannered dog.

That is why when I used to travel the dog show and field trial circuit (which took place in five Midwestern States), the circuit motels and hotels advertised, "Your dogs are always welcome. But their owners are subject to disqualification!"

Joyce - Bill, wouldn't it have been better to learn about Brandy's strong will-to-power in an earlier class? Then I could have been working on the change.

Trainer - You have.

Joyce - How?

Trainer - By requiring a proper "heel" and by timing. Like an Army drill sergeant you have been originating his every move. That placed you in charge of him. With persistence you have whittled him down by giving him attention and praise only when he tried to please you.

It all contributed to the role change of who responds to whom. Right now he is watching you, waiting for your next move. You are not fighting him. Yes, you have been working on his will-to-power from the first week.

That is why I am always saying, "Watch your timing and your body language. Require proper heeling. Don't fight them, let them fight themselves. Praise only the willingness.

Let's do some work.
Forward.
Halt.

Give them a "sit-stay" and walk away. If you have some doubts, stay within the Gotcha Zone. Otherwise walk all around the ring. Return to them. Pick up the leash with your right hand. Now praise in unison. "Good boy. Good girl," pat, pat, tidbit. Remember to make the training session pleasurable.

Forward.
About turn.
Fast.
Slow.
Normal.
Halt.
Forward.
Halt.

Give them a "stay." Keep the leash in your hand and stand out in front for a recall.

Ready. . .call your dogs.

That's the way. Have them sit in front of you. Now give the "stay" raising your left hand in the air for the palm signal. Turn around and go back out. Remember to have your dog come quickly, run backward, then stop suddenly giving the command to sit, which they should take verbally.

Carol - Question, Bill. What if my dog doesn't take the verbal "sit?"

Trainer - Then you should hold off the recall and practice the "heel-sit," saying "sit" each time you stop.

Ready, class. . .call your dogs.

Have them sit. Give them a "stay," turn around and do it again going back to where you started. I will travel around in case you need help.

Rena, move a little faster when you go backward for the recall. That's better. You want your dog to come in quickly.

Rena - Since I'm not going to be showing him, is that necessary?

Trainer - Yes. By having him respond quickly, you have better control over him. Also, when they come in fast, they do not do any ground

161

sniffing which distracts them from the exercise and shows poor control.

Ben, for competitive showing, let's demonstrate a little more class. After you say "Rommel," pause for the count of three, then give the "come" command. This is the type of control judges like to see. A willing working dog coming on the command, not the name.

Frank, you are trying to drag your dog to you. Mac's will and temper are causing him to resist the forcefulness. Do you have some treats with you?

Frank - No. I still don't like the idea that I have to use them to get him to do something for me.

Trainer - I'd like to see if he will respond to some. May I have him for a minute? Hmmm... All I can say, Frank, is although you don't like the idea, ol' Mac sure does. He must have read Pavlov's book. Why not be a little more flexible in training him?

A constant forceful approach will only turn him sour, which he is expressing already. How would you prefer to be trained if you were him?

Frank - Never thought of it that way. Got some treats to spare?

Trainer - Sure. Let me show you how to erase his sourness and slow responses. Fortunately, he is a "temperament" dog, not a "temperamental" one. Stand in front of him and give Mac a couple of pieces of meat to turn him on. Now offer him a piece of it and start running backwards giving him some more treats. Now stop, say "sit" and give him additional treats with the verbal and shoulder-pat praise. See? He forgot about the unpleasantness of the exercise already. Do this for a few days. Remember to do it in unison.

Within a week's time you will not need to use the treats, just the verbal or physical praise. Occasionally, give him a goodie. Would you care to demonstrate this for the class?

Frank - I'll give it a go.

Trainer - Class, may I have your attention. Frank is going to show you a method of using tidbits for changing Mac's attitude toward the recall exercise. So, please return to the "heel" position and give your dogs a "down-stay" command.

Frank, first demonstrate how slow Mac does the recall. Then use the tidbit.

"Tidbit" Recall

What Frank did was desensitize Mac's other responses to the recall. Remember to reinforce the responses you desire and let the other ones fade away. Repetition with the proper training methods will produce the desired responses in the dog's behavior.

Now I will demonstrate what is called the "finish" for those who wish to do it. This is used for A.K.C. trials. There are two ways to do it.

One way is to have your dog walk around behind you and sit in the "heel" position. The weakness in this method is that, when the dog gets behind you, he can stand there and not complete the exercise. I have seen this happen in shows.

I prefer the method where the dog turns around in front of me. This way I can keep my eyes on him all the time.

Now with your dog facing you, take the leash with your left hand and give the "heel" command. Step backward with your left foot and, at the same time, arch your dog in a loop effect.

As his head is being turned around to face the same direction you are, bring your left leg and the dog back to the forward position. Place the left foot back alongside the right one and, at the same time, give the command "sit." Any questions?

May I borrow Sheba? Watch how it's done. With Sheba it's necessary to take a big step backward while arching wide. With your smaller dogs, take a smaller step.

There, Mary, she's started for you.

For those who are not going to teach this part, give your dogs a "down-stay."

The rest of you, practice on your own. I will walk around to assist. After you have done one finish, give a "stay" and do the finish part again. No recalls.

John, be more sincere with your praise.

Jackie, you are starting to develop a problem with your dog to turn around. It's done with a circle effect rather than a triangle.

Be sure to say "stay," before you leave your dog, Joan.

Less firmness, Von. Baron is a sensitive dog. Fortunately though, he's not temperamental.

Class... That's enough practicing. Return to the "heel" position.

Finish

a.

b.

c.

d.

Let's all face in the counter-clockwise direction.
Forward.
Halt.
Down your dogs. Give them a "stay" and break in place.
Mary, would you please share the question you asked me earlier?

Mary - Yes. I wanted to know, since I'm going to enter A.K.C. obedience, which foot I should start off with when heeling. You said my right foot, but I always thought it was supposed to be the left one.

Trainer - Right. The common practice is to say the dog's name, pause, then step off with your left foot. Always.

I have found the method of using the dog's name with a pause conditions slower, hesitant responses.

I do not use the dog's name nor do I put in a pause. I merely say "heel" and step off with my right foot. This gives a "no-lag" heel step-off. Remember, the "heel" command does not mean movement. It means the dog's body is properly positioned on your left side. Of course, when you are walking, your dog walks alongside of you, always maintaining this shoulder to thigh position. Also, your dog is not to move or be moving if you are not moving. He will be sitting.

While you have one foot in motion, he will have to be in motion, too. The second you start, he starts. The second you stop, he stops. (Even to the point of split-second sits.)

This is precision training, the level of accomplishment any competitive obedience handler should strive for. The tougher the competition, the better the performance and the more highly trained the dog should be.

By keeping up this type of training program, breeders, in my opinion, can in only a few generations genetically restructure the mental abilities in their line of dogs, making them alert, quick and willing to work and please.

Let me demonstrate right-foot-step-offs with a dog that is obedience trained for A.K.C. shows. I'll be right back. . .

Now watch. I will give the "heel" command and step off with my left foot. Did you notice how she waited until she saw a movement before she started to move?

Now watch, when I start off with my right foot. With her head slightly in front of me, she saw my right foot moving forward. This activated her motoric nerves and started her movement. So by the time my left leg moved forward, she was right with it without any lag. I will do it again. Watch how the "heel" command makes her alert.

Heel. Good girl. You're finished. Let's go back to your run.

Right Foot   Step-Off

When starting off with the right foot, you give a body signal to your dog which is also a cue.

Does anyone know what this is? Well, I'll demonstrate with my invisible dog, Spook. Since you can't see him, you will have to watch only me because I'm the one who is going to signal.

Spook is on my left side. The judge says, "Forward." (By the way, Mary, remind me about this "forward" command for you.) I say "heel" and step off. There, did anyone catch it? I'll do it again. My feet are together. I give the command and step off. How's that? You should have caught it that time because I put a little more emphasis on it. Rena?

Rena - I believe you shifted your body to the left.

Trainer - Correct. In order to step off it is necessary to shift my body weight to the other foot. The dog sees the cue signal, then the right foot going forward activates his movement. So by the time you move your left leg forward, he is already moving forward with you. There is no lag when starting off with the "heel" command.

To take advantage of using the right-foot-step-off, develop your timing. Keep your dog's attention, because he has to see the right foot take-off.

While training wear soft shoes. Remove any metal tags (or tape them together so they don't jangle). Keep your training session short and sweet, and don't be afraid to use tidbits.

Joyce - What about when you stop? Do you use the same foot?

Trainer - I have found for most breeds that stopping on either foot results in the same quickness. However, for the large breeds and some small ones I prefer to stop on my left foot first, bringing the right one up alongside it.

Remember, the "heel" command does not mean movement. When your dog no longer sees your feet moving, he is supposed to stop and sit. I'll show you with Spook.

We're walking along and the judge gives the command "Halt." I stop on my left foot, which also supports my body weight. Remember, it is shoulder to thigh. I do a slight pause, then move my right foot alongside my left.

The important thing is that I do not shift my weight to my right foot which would be body-signaling for a continuous forward movement. This helps prevent the dog from drifting or sitting in front of you. Also, he is starting to sit while your right foot (which he cannot see) is still in motion. This is very helpful for a slow sitter.

These little "precision edges" have helped me to win run-offs in obedience trials. For those who are not familiar with A.K.C. trials, it is when two handlers have the same score and one is needed to be higher than the other for placement in the top scores. The judge has both of you in the ring together, then informs you that there is a tie score and he needs to place one dog over the other. This does not affect your original score and is considered only for winning placements.

The judge gives a "forward" command at which time you both step off. Then a "halt" is given. The dog who heels and sits the fastest wins.

Carol - Bill, do you have any more obedience trial tips for us?

Trainer - Certainly. Here's how to increase your dog's attention span once he has mastered the "sit-stay" command.

When you leave him with a "stay," walk around him in a 30 or 40 foot circle repeating "stay" (approximately 8 or 10 times) all the while. If he starts to look in another direction, repeat the "stay" command keeping his attention on you. Upon returning praise immediately to reinforce his watching you. This method will also enhance his responses to your commands.

I will demonstrate another show edge with a dog. I'll be right back. . .

This is Arnold. He is just about 10 months old and almost ready for obedience trials. Let me give him a wake-up, warm-up for a few minutes.

Now I will show you an off-leash finish exercise. Watch, "heel."

Ben - Wow! How did you ever get him to jump up, spin in the air, and land in the "heel" position like that?

Trainer - Easy, Ben. I'll do it again. "Heel, good boy!" See? All you have to do is say "heel."

Ben - Great! Seriously now, how did you train him to do that? Or did he just do it naturally?

Trainer - Arnold was trained to do it. I call it a "jump-finish."

I'm sure, this little trick saved the day at an obedience show once when I was handling a client's dog in the ring. The dog was a Great Pyrenees. The temperature that day was in the high seventies which was getting too warm for the big dog.

I had found out early in her training that she didn't work as well in hot weather as she did in cooler temperatures.

We managed to get through with all of her exercises that day, but it was as though she were moving in slow motion. By the time we got around to the final exercise, the recall, I knew she has had it. I gave her a "stay," walked away, turned, and gave her a mental "come" command using my eye contact. She finally came and stood in front of me. I glared at her and she sat.

The judge said, "Finish." I gave her the "heel" command, and all 120 pounds jumped up and spun in the air landing in the "heel" position. She collapsed to the ground, then struggled back up to a "sit" position.

When the judge said, "Exercise finished," the audience applauded her performance. I like to think her jump-finish saved us and helped to earn a leg for her C.D. that day.

Before you teach your dog the jump-finish command, you need to have the regular recall and finish down pat. I would say, for the average dog four weeks should be enough conditioning. You want to instill their finish off-leash, because to teach this, you need to use your right foot. If you start too soon, it could produce a poor finish. Your dog will stop and sit too far out from you.

Remember, good training is done progressively. Like climbing a ladder, be sure that each exercise is thoroughly instilled in order to support the next one.

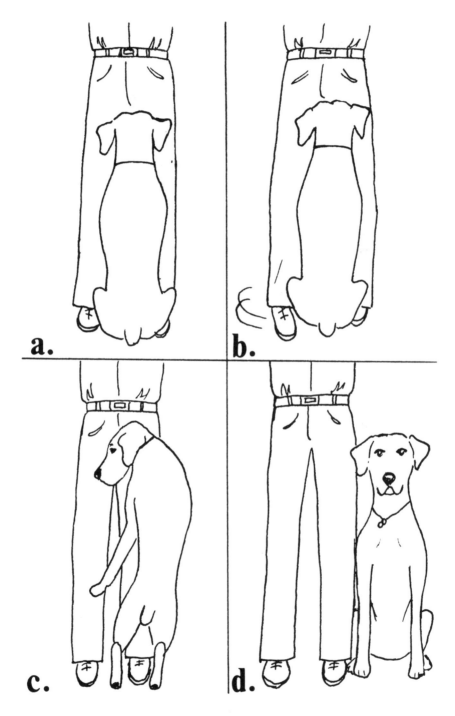

a.

b.

c.

d.

Watch how the jump-finish is done with Arnold. To demonstrate it, I will not give the "heel" command. This way, you will be able to see his reaction rather than his response to my command.

I have him sit in front of me. Now to get the spring-jump in his movement, when I say "heel," I take my right foot, and with the side of my shoe I give him a tap on his left side, as close to the floor as possible. This induces him to jump, for he wants to get clear of my foot. Watch closely. (Do this on leash.)

You do not want to kick him. Use proper timing, saying "heel" and using your foot in unison. Practice for a while without the dog.

Put a shoe in front of you and develop your timing. Have your foot make contact with the floor a few inches before making contact with the shoe (a slight sliding effect). This prevents you from accidentally doing a kick. Once you have mastered it, then teach it to your dog.

I will repeat, do not teach this until you have instilled the finish and you have mastered the "foot-slide."

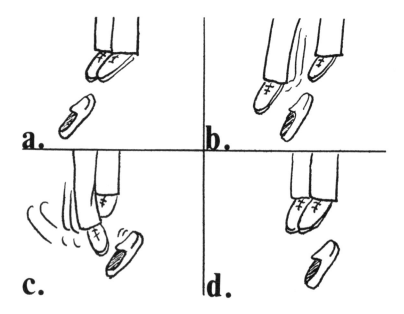

Carol - How much force should we put in the tap?

Trainer - It will depend upon your dog's sensitivity. Use the same basic method as for all other exercises. Use only the degree of force necessary to get the desired result.

When practicing with the shoe, a three to four inch movement is a gauge for the force needed on the average dog. Remember to return your right foot next to the left, after you make contact with the dog.

Jackie - I would like to know how to get faster sits for obedience competition.

Trainer - Okay. There are several ways to get a dog to sit quickly. Here is one of my favorite methods. First, make sure your dog is doing the automatic sits consistently in the normal walk exercise. Next, practice halting during the fast exercise. The sits are quickened by using a snap-release backward on a 45 degree angle, and also giving the command "sit." This is done every time you stop, even though the dog knows it already and is sitting automatically. Once he is doing split second sits, I praise verbally, physically, and with a tidbit. I keep up this fast heeling and sitting for about 5 minutes a day until I have a conditioned response pattern.

Any more questions? Don't be bashful. This is our last week together. The next time we meet, it might be under competition.

Ben - Bill, I noticed one thing. When you turn the corner, Arnold seems to square off rather than arch around it. Is that something he is doing on his own, or is it another one of your professional trade secrets?

Trainer - It has been up to now. Like the jump-finish, it's a showmanship edge over my competitors. Since you weren't bashful, I'll answer your question.

Arnold was conditioned to square his corners rather than curve them.

Again, know your dog. Have his respect, willingness to please and trust, before you use this method. If your dog is somewhat fearful or shy, work it out ahead of time. I will demonstrate with Arnold.

For a right turn, place the left foot in front of you, and as you pivot on the ball of the foot, turn to the right. The right foot comes into action and bumps the dog's right rump. This makes him want to get out of the way of the bump contact. So he moves his rear end to the left. This then creates more of a 90 degree turn than a curve. I will do it again.

Remember to use only the degree of force necessary to get the response you want. When the dog is doing it, stop using the foot bump and give the praise reward.

Ben - What about the left turns? You can't use your feet for that.

Trainer - No, the left turns are conditioned a little differently. I use a thin 1/4 inch wooden dowel rod. As I turn to my left and am squaring off my corners, I tap his left rump with the rod at the same time. This causes him to react, moving his rear away from the tap making it go to the right.

In practicing the left turns, you will have to correlate your foot work in turning and using the dowel rod tap. Perfect timing is necessary for the left turn. Watch how it is done.

I take a shorter step with my right pivoting on it while turning to the left. Then I step off with my left. I also use a slight body cue leaning to my right side when turning.

I do not hold the leash with my left hand. I keep the rod close to my side. This way ,the rod is not menacing to him.

I will repeat: *KNOW YOUR DOG'S DEMEANOR BEFORE USING THIS METHOD.* Some dogs are more sensitive than others.

Sometimes, I will hide the rod up my sleeve so it will not spook the dog as we are walking. I let it slide down for the left turn, after which I pull it back up, out of the dogs view. You do not want to threaten your dog with it. You just want to condition a surprise reaction response to the tap.

I will be back in a minute after I put Arnold up.

Mary, before I forget, Sheba steps off when she hears my "forward" command. So when you practice at home, have a friend start you off heeling using a different phrase, such as "start walking."

I have seen some handlers do beautifully in practice or fun trials. Yet when under the pressure of competitive trials, it appeared that neither the dog nor the handler had enough training. (Poor heeling, sloppy sits, no sits, refusal on the recall, walking away from the group stays, etc.)

I sometimes asked my clients what their thoughts were. "Oh, I was nervous because I was watching my competition. Some were so perfect, and I just got tensed up. I didn't think my dog would obey me on the first command."

Yes, the person was right. The dog didn't obey the first command.

Attitude, especially in the show ring, is very important. Assume a positive attitude and you will find yourself getting more positive results.

As far as watching the competition, it is advisable to find a quiet corner away from the ring. Going by the number sequence, you can time yourself as to when you are up, or have a friend give you 5 or 10 minutes notice.

No dog is number one until the last exercise is finished!

Be positive in your thoughts. Thoughts affect both your emotions and your physical body signals, which our canine friends are capable of tuning in to. Thoughts are things. *JUST DO YOUR BEST AND LET THE JUDGE DO THE REST*!

Most importantly, relax. It's not life or death, just a dog show. There's always another one right around the corner.

I would like to give you some special commands now, which can be used for home or show.

The "kennel" command is used when you want your dog to enter an enclosure such as a car, show crate, kennel run, or room.

Let's say, you want your dog to go into the rear of your station wagon. You stand about six feet away, give a "sit-stay" command, and open the rear door. Take a leash and say "kennel." Take a few quick steps and encourage your dog to jump in. It may be necessary for you to climb in with a fearful dog at first and give him a tidbit. A directional hand signal can be given along with the command.

Now suppose you have your dog in the car and do not want him to get out when you open the door. The command I use for this is simply "stay in there." It means just that.

As you open the door and start to get out, tell him "nein" several times (or use "no"), pause, then say "stay in there." Give him a tap on the nose at the same time, if necessary, to reinforce the command. Do this several times, until the dog does not come out when you open the door. He should wait for your "come" or release command.

This can also be used in teaching the dog to stay in a particular room at home. Tell him to "kennel" into the room you want him to be in. If he starts to follow you out, say "nein/no" several times, then say "stay in there."

With this method you can establish territorial boundaries right inside the home.

Jackie - Why not just say "stay?"

Trainer - When confining a dog to a given area, he should be allowed movement within that area. When you give the "stay" command, your dog is required to hold whatever position he is in, be it standing, sitting, or lying down. This is impractical for the home and difficult (if not impossible) for the car.If you say "stay," it puts your dog in the position where he would have to break the command. That, of course, weakens his responses and undermines your control over him.

John - Bill, suppose I want my hunting dog to stay in the rear of the station wagon. I have been advised to either crate him or put up a wire-mesh guard to keep him behind the rear seats. But either of these methods prevent him from protecting my belongings when I leave the car.

Trainer - Yes, it is ironic. The gate indicates a protective dog. Yet like a lion in a zoo, he can't do anything.

Your dog can be more effective if he can move freely when necessary. For this purpose I have a "back" command, which eliminates the need for a crate or wire fence.

Here's how it's done. Always put him in and take him in and out from the tailgate. Do not let him in the side door, so that he has to walk on the rear seat. Once he is in the rear area, close the tailgate and window. Get into the rear seat and try to entice him over by slapping the bottom seat. Make any kind of sounds you wish, just be sure you do not use any commands.

The second he falls for it and begins to climb over, give him a firm correction and say, "back, back," along with a tap on his nose or paws. If he manages to get over, push him back over repeating "back" several times. Repeat this five or six times giving the "back" command, whenever he starts to climb over.

Back

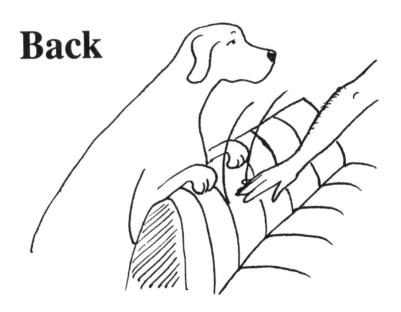

Now leave him in the car and walk around behind a building and watch him for five minutes or so. If he begins to climb over, get to him immediately and correct him. Be sure, you do not approach him hurriedly which could condition fear.

Remember always to approach your dog cool, calm and collected.

Once he has accepted this invisible barrier, return, open the tailgate, and give him a praise reward and take him out.

This exercise should be practiced and mastered at home before you head for the open road. One thing I should mention. If your hunting dog is being trained to the "back" retrieve command, use a different command for "back" in the station wagon.

John - Hey Bill, I thought you said before, never trick a dog.

Trainer - Right you are. I still maintain that tricking your dog haphazardly will create negative results by making him mistrustful of you. But there are exceptions to every rule. In this case, we are using a trick for a specific positive result.

The dog learns not to be conned into violating your original command. This is very effective in that most dogs catch on quickly and will not allow themselves to be tricked again.

I want to introduce just one more new exercise. But before we start, let's review. This is important.

Always put your dog through the exercises he knows before teaching him anything new. This reinforces the previous training and helps open up his response system. So pick up your leashes. .

Forward.
Slow.
Normal.
About turn.
Stand your dog.
Circle your dogs and back out front.

Return, praise.
Forward.
Halt.

Now I will demonstrate what I call the "watch" command. This command may be used for the home watch dog, for conformation, field training, and water retrieving.

May I borrow Jerome? First, I will introduce him to some liverwurst. Now I will give him a "stand-stay" and stand a few feet in front of him, with the leash in the right hand, the left hand is held in a 45 degree angle position, with the index finger pointing straight out. Give the command "watch" and, at the same time, move your hand so that the index finger is pointing straight up. Bring your hand back to the starting 45 degree position, then back to the vertical and repeat, "Watch, watch, watch," each time you move your hand.

If your dog is not paying attention to your hand movement, tease him with a tidbit while repeating both hand and verbal watch signals. After the third or fourth time, give him the treat.

This command helps develop their attentiveness which enhances all training. Remember, you need their attention for at least 3 or 4 seconds in order for them to absorb the commands.

Carol - Jerome seems to respond to the tidbit much better for you than for me. Why?

Trainer - Possibly you have the tidbit just given to him. If you noticed, I teased him with it a few times letting him smell it and lick it. I didn't let him have it immediately. When he gave me a more enthusiastic response, he then got a small (about 1/2 inch square) piece.

Once you have conditioned this response, you do not need to use the tidbits anymore. For most dogs, your verbal or physical praise is their reward.

Watch

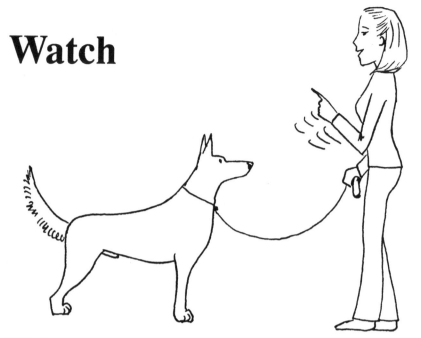

Watch
(retrieving)

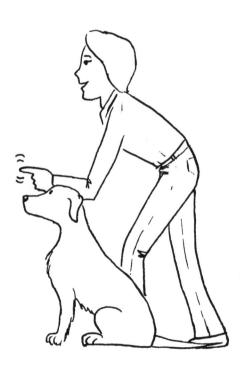

John - How can the "watch" command be used for duck hunting?
Trainer - First get Dusty to respond to your hand signals. Then have him sit alongside of you. Place your left hand by the right side of his face. Extend the index finger, give the "watch" command, point straight ahead, and move your hand up and down a couple of inches only.

Once he is looking in the direction you are pointing, have another person throw the retrieving bumper, so that it lands in line with the "watch" direction. Then have your dog retrieve it.

For the left angle retrieve, again place your extended finger alongside his face giving it a tap or two, so that he will turn his head left. At that time, signal for the bumper toss.

Do the same for the right angle retrieve, only this time tap the right side of his face and move your hand to the right, so that he will follow it. Once you have mastered this, you can then give the watch command pointing to an incoming flight of ducks, thus preparing him for shooting and retrieving.

There are no real mysteries to training, just understanding is necessary. Practically all dogs can be trained.

By observing a dog's behavior, we can gain that needed understanding. Remember, the pupil can only be raised to the level of his teacher.

"To desire is to obtain. To aspire is to achieve.

Achievement of whatever kind is the crown of effort, the diadem of thought."

(James Allen, *As A Man Thinketh*, Brownlow Publishing Company)

So let's put our right foot forward and step into a new dimension of relationship with our canine companions.

Pleasure not pain is the name of the game. Like the symbolic flood, let's reproach and cleanse our thinking of some outdated methods of training.

Hey! I've put all the dogs to sleep!

FORWARD

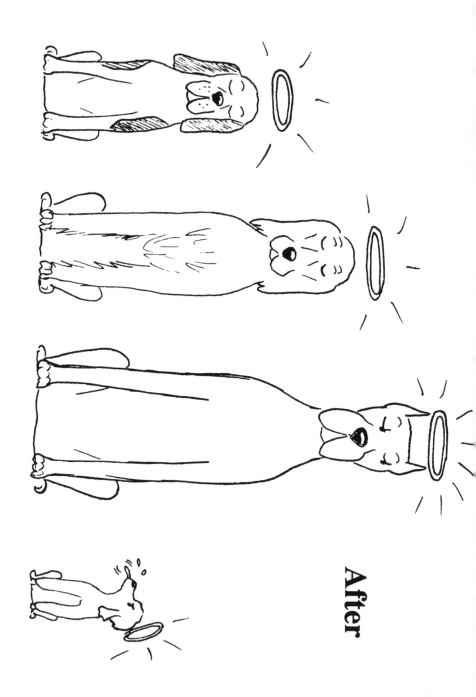

After

V.

TESTIMONIES . . .
FOR DOUBTING THOMASES

The following interview took place in September 1990 between Joan Guertin, owner of COMMON SENSE DOG TRAINING in Carmichael, California, and Marta Bowes, owner of the female Golden Retriever Emma. It reflects a typical case history of a dog ruined with forceful techniques and salvaged with psychological training concepts.

Joan Guertin became a trainer with the German Shepherd Dog Club in Phoenix in the early '60s, where she taught her own training classes. Over the years, she used the methods recommended by experts, but did not feel very good about some of their forceful techniques.

After she read in 1985 my first book, *Hows and Whys of Psychological Dog Training*, she learned to understand why dogs will respond to a challenge with a challenge and to respect with respect.

Using my psychological approach she has successfully retrained dogs with serious behavior problems, such as Emma.

MARTA   EMMA   JOAN

183

TRAGIC BUT TRUE...
WITH A HAPPY ENDING

Joan - What was Emma's problem?
Marta - Emma had a history diagnosed by experts as dominant aggressive behavior.

Joan - At what age did you obtain Emma and what was the puppy's behavior after you took her home?
Marta - I got her at the age of seven weeks. She was very active and also, she took lots of naps the first few weeks. But every time I was with her, she mostly chewed on me. Because of this it got to the point, where I did not enjoy spending much time with her anymore. I was also experiencing scratches from her nails. Increasingly, her activities consisted of scratching, chewing, and biting. I cannot say that our interactions were very pleasant.

Joan - How did you deal with this aggressive play?
Marta - Most of the time, by telling her "no" and pushing her away. Unfortunately, I wasn't getting anywhere with that. Therefore, I looked forward to starting her in a puppy class, once she would be three months old. This was recommended by my veterinarian. She was not accepted for training before that time.

Joan - So, she just went unchecked in terms of her dominant aggressive type of play. You were the pincushion, right?
Marta - Yes, but not totally, because I ended up contacting the trainer ahead of time who was giving the class. I thought I could get advise from him as to what to do until the classes began.

Joan - What was his advice?
Marta - It was to use banishment as a form of punishing her.

Joan - Define banishment, how did you banish her?
Marta - It was suggested that I should isolate her. I used the bathroom for this purpose. So when she got out of hand, and when she was constantly chewing and wouldn't stop, she was placed in the bathroom. The periods of time lasted up to twenty minutes. I was

advised to lengthen the time, until I got the required response from her. If she immediately started chewing again, after I let her out, then she was supposed to go back in.

Joan - What did you accomplish by this?
Marta - As far as I could tell nothing, except a reprieve for those few minutes from her constant aggressive behavior. Other than giving me a break, the bathroom isolation didn't seem to curb the misbehavior itself.

Joan - Where there any physical reprimands? Did you shake her or anything like that?

Marta - Yes, I did that, too. This was also recommended by the trainer of the puppy class. I picked her up by the scruff of the neck, shook her, saying with a loud voice "no." This, I was told, was what the mother dog did with her puppies in the litter, in order to corrected them.

Joan - Did the misbehavior decrease?
Marta - Unfortunately not. Initially, she tried to dig in where ever she was and resisted as much as she could, in order not to be isolated. The final confrontation was a few month later, when I was going to banish her in the bathroom again. She snapped at me, when I grabbed her collar to drag her toward the bathroom, although we were not even close to it at that point. I am sure, she knew my intention.

Joan - How did you deal with her snapping at you?
Marta - I got very angry and yelled at her. I stood her up, grabbed her underneath her front legs and walked her in on her back legs to the bathroom. I threw her in there and closed the door.

Joan - What was the recommendation when you mentioned the snapping behavior to the trainer?
Marta - I was advised to hang her.

Joan - Describe, what was meant by hanging.

Marta - That consisted of putting a choke chain collar and a leash on her, and somehow standing at a height, so I could be above her, and pulling up, so she would be suspended by the collar and then choked.

Joan - Off the floor?
Marta - Yes.

Joan - What was the result, when you tried the hanging?
Marta - Because of her weight it was difficult for me to do it. I was unsuccessful the first three times and seemed to subdue her on the fourth. However, I did not see any immediate change in her behavior afterwards. The relationship did not seem different. Although I did the hanging, I didn't feel good about it at all when I did it.

Joan - How did Emma perform in the puppy class?
Marta - Every time, after we had practiced a new activity in class, she would throw up when we returned to our position. In order to avoid that, just before the class I sedated her with a tranquilizer my veterinarian had prescribed for this purpose.

Joan - This is pathetic. Were there any incidents within the puppy class where your dog exhibited dominant aggressive behavior?
Marta - No. In fact she was submissive. One of her litter mates, her sister, happened to be in the class we took. Her sister was dominant and Emma was submissive. There was never a question about it. Emma, when confronted, would always either crouch or lie down and roll over. It was very obvious that she was the one that always backed off.

Joan - At this time, did you receive any other type of advise from the professional trainer or from the veterinarian in terms of correcting your dog?
Marta - I was supposed to apply the dominant-aggressive techniques that were used in class and constantly practice and reinforce them. The conclusion was, that Emma was pretty hard-headed. At the end of class, the suggestion was made by the trainer and also the vet to have

Emma evaluated by the Behavior Department of a California Veterinary College and to get specific instructions from them.

Joan - What was you experience at the Veterinary College? Did you consult with a canine behaviorist there? Would you like to describe your sessions?

Marta - Emma was tested and evaluated and they felt, that she was very strong-willed, and that she had aggressive behavior tendencies that needed to be dealt with immediately.

Joan - Were your advisors veterinary students or the director of the program?

Marta - I saw the department head every time. There were also anywhere from two to four students sitting in on each visit. It was a group discussion. Suggestions were made from different people. At the end of the visit I would receive their recommendations in writing, and I would have sort of a written prescription of things I should try.

Joan - You were getting advise from a number of different people, although the director was there and was sanctioning the suggestions, correct?

Marta - Yes, he was definitely active in it.

Joan - What were the suggestions or training methods you were given to curb her behavior?

Marta - The first thing we worked with was a special collar called the "Gentle Leader." Emma had to wear it one week straight without taking it off. A very short lead of approximately 18 inches was hanging from it. Thus, I could correct her at any time without fear of being bitten.

Joan - Did this make any appreciable difference in her behavior?

Marta - Yes, it did at that time. But my concern was what would happen once it was removed? After the first week, she wore the collar only during the day time. It was removed for the night.

Joan - What did it actually solve?

Marta - The main thing it solved was that it took away fear on my part. I could correct her without fear, whenever she exhibited unwanted behavior. I only felt safe with her when she had it on. They explained to me, that when I controlled her with the "Gentle Leader," I was setting the tone and showed her that I was in charge and dictated the relationship.

Joan - What were some of the other behavioral corrections recommended to you? Incidently, was she still snapping and biting at you? Did she growl, snap, bite, or do anything aggressive when you put the "Gentle Leader" on?

Marta - No. I didn't have trouble putting it on her, and she wore it for quite awhile. Yet, I did not have complete faith in the fact that once it was removed, it was supposed to carry over.

Joan - So you stopped using it?

Marta - No, I used it as directed. She was gradually weaned from it. However, we still were not at a point where you could say the results were satisfactory, or the problems had been solved. So I continued to go back and see them for more input and suggestions.

Joan - In the meantime, were you still using banishment? And were you still getting the same results when you reached for the collar?

Marta - I still used banishment at that time. I remember that later on, she didn't snap at me, but she would wrinkle her nose and bare her teeth. That happened and continued for quite sometime.

Joan - What other suggestions did you receive from the Veterinary College?

Marta - I received specific suggestions for specific behaviors. For instance, for jumping to bump my knee in her chest. I also was told to take her back to obedience training. So we repeated the puppy class with the same trainer with whom we had taken it initially.

Joan - The first time you took her to the Veterinary College was October 8, 1987. By January 1988, she exhibited a new behavior. She was challenging you for territory. Is this correct?

Marta - Yes, when I wanted her to get off a living room chair and another time off my bed, she growled, wrinkled her nose, bared her teeth and snapped at me.

After relating this story to my advisors at the Veterinary College, I was told to get a rubber hose, actually to get a long piece, have it cut in certain lengths and have them distributed all over the house. The next time she exhibited this kind of behavior, I should reprimand her and strike her across the nose with the rubber hose.

Joan - Did this treatment have a desirable result?
Marta - There were no dramatic changes. However, one time when I hit her across the nose with the rubber hose, she yelped and looked like I had flattened her eye. It turned out that it was her second eyelid that was coming up. I had somehow hit part of her eye.

From the beginning, I wasn't comfortable using this form of training. But after that, I felt like an ogre and couldn't continue with it anymore.

Joan - Did you stop then seeing the experts at this Veterinary College?
Marta - I saw them one more time, which was just for a final tie-up of things. That was it. They thought the dog was okay now. I never felt that the problems were fully resolved. I had followed through with what I was asked to do. But I didn't have total trust and faith in Emma after all. Because of the methods I had to use, I never knew what her reaction would be.

Joan - Was she still challenging you?
Marta - Sometime later something came up again. But in general, she had stopped. It was still suggested that I enroll in more obedience classes, because she needed the constant reminder and the constant regimen of a class like this.

Joan - So you went to a regular obedience class, and with what results?
Marta - Pretty much the same results that we had experienced all along, which was that we were usually the worst in the class. There were certain commands that she would sometimes perform or not. She

was never good at staying, whether it was "sit-stay" or "down-stay." We would get past the first couple of classes, then we would be left behind, while everyone else continued to move forward.

Also, I felt that over the period of time we went to training classes, an adversative relationship had developed. Instead of working together, it was a constant clash of the wills. I had been told to sit on this dog, and that I needed to get control of her, which I did not have.

Joan - What methods of training were used? How would you describe the training?

Marta - It was dominance training also, but it was not as severe as in the puppy classes. Again, the trainer pointed out that I must let her know and feel who is the boss. Sometimes, when the trainer saw that the dog did not follow my commands, she would try it. She would walk up to Emma grab her around the neck, shake her, and reprimand her by saying "no" with a forceful voice. This did not help much either. So it was not just me.

Joan - On the "sit-stays," were you able to leave the dog, or did she grab your leg and try to stay with you? In other words, did she suffer anxiety when you tried to leave her on a long sit?

Marta - Yes. I have never been able to get any distance away from her without her constantly inching forward or just absolutely getting up and moving. She pretty much stayed next to me. Even turning her over to an instructor did not change anything. No one had been successful at making her do what they wanted, whether it was me or an instructor.

Joan - Shortly, after you had completed an obedience course, you contacted me because you still had problems with heeling and sit-stays. I invited you for a private session with the dog.

Marta - I was still pretty frustrated because I did not have control over Emma, whether it was going for a walk or attempting to get any sort of behavior I wanted from her. I became interested in your approach when I read about it. I made an appointment with you to have Emma evaluated, to find out where this dog was emotionally at this point.

I have to admit, I was very much surprised that Emma responded to you in a totally different way then she had done before with anyone else. From the beginning, she was very responsive, and there was an instant rapport. I had always been sure that she was not stupid and knew the commands, but for reasons unknown to me, would not exhibit the behavior requested of her. Obviously, there was something very different in your approach with her, since she was so responsive.

Joan - Up to this time, how long had you been working with Emma to get the results that you had finally achieved?

Marta - Well, I had spent about a year to train her. I had gone through three 6-week puppy classes, one 6-week obedience class, plus six visits to the Behavioral Department of the Veterinary College. Also, we were working just about every day on exercises and commands.

Joan - She came to me March 15, 1989. We did four to six private sessions.

Marta - Yes, I then attended one of your group classes.

Joan - While you were working with me, using a gentle, non-aggressive approach to training, did you see any concrete changes?

Marta - Yes, I did. A lot of positive changes happened not only in the dog but also in me. I had to re-consider my whole position that had been battered into me. I had been brainwashed that the only way to control my dog was to prove to her with physical force who was the boss. Therefore, it took a lot of retraining on my part, more than anything else, to initiate new non-aggressive patterns and new positive behaviors in myself when interacting with Emma.

In addition to this attitudinal change resulting in a different relationship with Emma, I received many useful suggestions which were helpful in specific situations.

Joan - Can you remember any of those suggestions?

Marta - The "leave-it" command. Basically, she loves people and gets terrible excited when anyone enters, whether it is someone she knows or not. I usually had a leash on her, and was trying to restrain her with my weight against hers which was never successful. The "leave-it" command involved letting her have play in the leash. It gave her the responsibility of restraining herself. When I told her to "leave-it," she would be the one holding back and not lunging or fighting me.

Joan - Did you have to make any severe corrections in order to get these positive results?

Marta - No, because that was not part of the training program. One of the most important things I had to learn was not to get mad or frustrated when training. I learned in the whole process not to be so hard and not to expect perfection from her, i.e., to remain non-judgmental.

Joan - Any corrections you made were very gentle. Is this correct?

Marta - Yes, I did not get excited and talked quietly and sedately. But I was firm and consistent. Those were the important principles involved.

Joan - Were you ultimately able to get her to walk with you at the "heel" position, and were you able to do the "sit-stay?"

Marta - She heels on leash and also off-leash. I will drop the leash and walk with her. She knows what I expect from her and she pretty much stays. I can get her to sit-stay and walk away approximately six to eight feet. There are times when I am able to get further away. It still needs improvement, because it is not yet consistent.

I also feel, since our relationship was totally destroyed, it will take at least as much time to rebuild it as it took to tear it down.

Joan - Has there been any more of the aggressive behavior since you stopped acting aggressively toward the dog?

Marta - There was only one incident. Fortunately, I stopped myself in time. Almost one year ago, I attempted to take something from her which she was not supposed to eat. I could see that we were developing a confrontation situation. Rather then getting involved in an aggressive power struggle I simply told her to "leave-it." Although I had to repeat the command, she finally did it. I was amazed about this reaction considering that this dog will eat anything and everything given the chance. The most important thing was me remembering to back off, not to get mad, and to implement a whole different type of training to what I had done for the first year and one half of her life.

Joan - What was your gut feeling, when you had to reach out and be aggressive in your training?

Marta - I hated it. It was totally against everything I believed in. But I found no support for my belief system. When I used these aggressive methods, I reconciled myself to the fact that all these people who told me how train Emma knew what they were talking about, whether they were experts or not. Pretty much everyone, from the veterinarians to the trainers, to acquaintances was giving uniform advise consisting of "get tough, get harsher, be the boss." I wasn't achieving any success on my own and had no experience. So I followed their advise, since that was the only advise available to me.

Joan - This also brings up another point. It would be wonderful if people would listen more to their gut feeling. If you don't like what you are asked to do, to have the courage of your convictions and stop and search for other opinions and options, to look for a trainer that will work with you in a way you are comfortable with.

Marta - I would also suggest that it would be a good idea to observe training classes of anyone you are considering as a trainer. Unfortunately, I was getting the same advise over and over again. The only reason I was drawn to you was when I read something about your system that was different from what I had been encountering so far.

Joan - It probably said something to the effect that we were working to build a relationship based on mutual respect and trust instead of fear.

    When you were dealing with the other trainers and other training methods, from the sound of it, the dog was expected to do all the changing. Am I correct in that?

Marta - Yes. I was told that I had to make it very clear to my dog that I am in charge. I had physically to put her in her place. If I didn't do this at an early age, then my dog would be out of hand.

Joan - I always stress that it is necessary for the owner to make many changes rather than to put the full responsibility on the dog. In other words, becoming a responsible owner as well as having a dog that is responsible for his behavior.

The two of you have come a long way and I was delighted to be a part of it. I felt that when I first met you, I wasn't sure which one of you was more uptight, you or the dog. It has been a real pleasure to watch the changes in attitude, the growth, and to be able to look at this wonderful dog lying at my feet. She is relaxed, she is happy and responds almost instantly to a nice quiet voice. She appears to be a much happier dog. You seem to be much happier also.

Marta - You told me at the time that Emma was basically a dog that had been backed into a corner where she was fighting for her life. All her aggressive behavior was an act of survival. She was aggressive and snapped because she felt threatened. The very first time I saw you, you expressed your surprise, that she was not in worse shape considering what she had been through.

Joan - I was amazed at the strength of character of this dog, because all the things that had been done to her, would have by rights destroyed a dog of lesser character. In most instances, with traditional training we are really threatening the dogs. In the case of Emma we removed the threat and she advanced on her way to a normal dog.

When Marta would get discouraged, I would tell her to reach around and pat herself on the back. Because, a person less determined to solve the problem, would have taken the puppy to the pound or had it destroyed years ago. Marta was to be commended for her diligence, her stick-to-itiveness, her desire to really find a solution.

Marta - I didn't feel like there was any other choice. I was determined to have a good relationship with Emma. Hindsight always helped. I remember, that any time I did anything that was harsh, the sensation was as I said earlier that she would rebound as hard if not harder.

Joan - Obviously, bonding was lacking in your relationship. Many behaviorists will tell you that the bonding takes place within a brief period of time when the puppy is very young. The puppy bonding was non existent.

Do you feel that you have been able to establish a bond even though this dog is three or four years old now?

Marta - Yes. But it has taken a really long time on both sides of the bond. I feel more comfortable with her now than I ever have. I am sure that it has been the same for her. It is a rebuilding process that has come a long way, but I am sure we can take it even further than we have at this point.

Joan - How would you describe your relationship with Emma now and what direction are you going to take in her future training?

Marta - We still have a way to go, but it is definitely not adversative or confrontational at all. I enjoy her a lot more than I used to. In fact, before I felt annoyed a lot of the time, because it was constant work, it was never fun. I feel as though that has changed completely. I would like to continue working with what we have begun to build. I want to continue to emphasize respect and trust.

C.W. MEISTERFELD and EMMA

195

Author's Comment

I personally tested and evaluated Emma. She was very friendly, responsive and obedient and showed no signs of aggression or fear whatsoever. I feel very pleased that this beautiful dog was saved considering what she went through when her owner followed the written instructions she received from the Veterinary College which read as follows:

Behavioral Therapy

DIAGNOSIS: *Dominance related aggressive behavior.*

GENERAL EVALUATION: *Emma has made a little progress with affection control. Recently Emma growled and has been unruly. Gentle leader still offers good control. The goal is to implement an increase and begin very severe correction to deal with Emma's misbehavior.*

SPECIFIC INSTRUCTIONS:

1. *Find a rubber hose, wooden dowel or plastic toy bat wrapped with duct tape for correcting Emma. She should be rapped on the bridge of the nose, head or neck when she growls or threatens.*
2. *If possible, stage a situation where Emma is likely to be aggressive and correct her **immediately** if she growls or misbehaves. If she is good, make sure to praise her.*

READY, WILLING, ABLE

This brief statement is a synopsis of what I have been trying to achieve with my dogs for five years. I think I have found the answer with C. W. Meisterfeld's training philosophy.

I went with my dog to my local kennel club's obedience classes. I quit after three sessions when I was told that I would have to hurt her to get her to obey me. I didn't want to yell at my dog or jerk her by the chain collar to the point that she would be yelping with pain like other dogs so treated. We were actually told that this didn't really hurt. I thought it was gag and puke time.

If someone had put a chain around my neck, even one that would not slip, and asked me to heel and then snapped me good and hard, not only would they not get my obedience, they might very well have to run me down in order to put it on. And even then I might fight. I wouldn't tolerate that treatment anymore than any of you would. My five year old bitch was already sour on obedience, and my instinct told me that I didn't need to hurt her. Also, since I am not a violent person, I dropped out of the class.

My second experience involved my driving 60+ miles to a class that was "advanced" obedience. They were doing a much better job than the snatch and punish group. If they had been more focused, it might have worked very well. Our instructors herded us around and yelled, "sit" and "down" and did their best to demonstrate. But then we got off on individual instructors' likes, such as Schutzhund work. To the best of my limited knowledge, there is no exercise in AKC obedience which requires my dog to jump a jump, down on a heel, and jump a jump again.

The next time we left our dogs on sit-stays and down-stays and walked around the ring (could have been the cause of a major dog fight between all of the dogs).

I continued this class for the purpose of socialization and simply did not do the exercises that were not directly related to CD work.

Ultimately my Hustle did get her CD. However, she did it reluctantly and only because she knew it would please me did she work at all. There was not one shred of joy in it for her. There was no willingness. It was very disappointing for me since I had by then spent a year and a half with training. I became convinced that my dog just wasn't the working type. Maybe I really did need a Sheltie who reportedly are required to read the book at birth and perform accordingly. I knew that neither me nor the dog was lacking particularly in the brains department. Yet I felt that all of these instructors, who were touted to be experts and reportedly very successful, had to be wrong. I knew for sure that they were wrong for me and wrong for my dog. However, I did not know where to turn to for a better approach.

One day, a miracle happened. The breeder of my dog, Sylvia Hammarstrom, Skansen Kennels, sent me a copy of a book entitled *Jelly Bean vs. Dr. Jekyll and Mr. Hyde* by C.W. Meisterfeld. I could not believe it. I was extremely skeptical. Here was someone telling me I could have my working dog, and that she would be willing, ready, and able without fear, and without punishment. Here was someone who said I could be in charge without brutality. I called a few people. I talked endlessly to my breeder, who would probably rather never hear from me again, and I took the leap and bought every tape and book that C.W. Meisterfeld had available since his facility and mine are about 3300 miles apart.

Results: I read every line in the *Hows and Whys of Psychological Dog Training* at least three times (probably more like five or six times). I have listened to the tapes of his audio cassette albums *Canine Behavioral Psychology and Psychological Dog Training* while driving in my van for the past 2000 miles. I worked very hard to achieve the state of mind resulting in the conviction, "O.K. kid, you can do it!" It makes sense! It won't get done if you don't put the collar on the dog. By the way, I now have three bitches to work. Two of them I just got, one is a three year old who has always lived in a kennel - that should tell you something -and a four month old, barely leash-broken pup.

Since I purchased C.W. Meisterfeld's books and tapes I have been working with my dogs on a permanent basis. My older, sour dog is beginning to work with zest and vibrancy, a three year old bitch, only in training for four weeks, now is beginning to work off-lead having already accomplished the sits, downs, heeling, and stands for examination. Presently, we are working on "come front." I'm aiming at the Ocala show to go for her first leg on her CD. My five month old puppy is now doing her downs having already learned to heel, stand, stay, and sit.

I know this may not sound like much, but the three year old bitch was born in a kennel, was raised in a kennel and had never left that kennel before she came to me just two and a half months ago. Best of all, I have not raised my voice, yanked, jerked or threatened any of my dogs.

Handel wrote the Hallelujah Chorus that we are all familiar with, but Bill Meisterfeld wrote the "Work Them Chorus" and it works for me. My Giant Schnauzers are happy, I am happy and we are all just a bunch of monkeys in a barrel.

Be happy and enjoy life!

Barbara Schatt
Crescent, Florida

LESLIE J. HARDY, D.V.M.

This is to inform others of my high regard for C.W. Meisterfeld as originator of some highly innovative ideas in dog training. Within the last seven years, I personally have entrusted two dogs to him for training. For instance, he was able to turn a hyper neurotic Australian Shepherd into an obedient well-adjusted pet.

His message is to establish the all important master-dog relationship, the basis for any dog's psychological stability. Rather than conditioning obedience with fear, he advocates instilling mutual respect and trust between master and dog. This psychological balance is the cornerstone of his teaching.

Leslie J. Hardy, D.V.M., Park Centre Animal Hospital
Alameda, California

NAN AND COMPANIONS

I have been involved very seriously in Ibizan Hounds for over 17 years. Ibizans are generally non-aggressive and amendable, though independent. I never had any accidental breeding until our Catahoulax Heeler farm dog slipped in with Fenix our champion Ibizan Hound on the fifth day of her season. Somehow she managed to bring forth one pure white, blue eyed lump of a bitch puppy, known as Fcasco, or Moby pup.

I have always been interested in a lurcher, a dog with sight/hound skills but controllable like a herding dog. Fcasco was protectively mothered by Ashley until she was three weeks old at which time Ashley, like a teenage mother, grew bored, leaving Fcasco for me and the Ibizans to raise.

Fcasco grew into a handsome and intelligent dog, racy white body and ice blue eyes, but black nose. She was playful and bright. But at about one year of age she started fighting, mostly with her mother. This went beyond the normal struggle for rank in the pack. I tried traditional reprimands but the situation kept escalating. Fights were getting serious. I'd take her by the collar and shake her, yelling in her face. This only seemed to excite her more. Fcasco walked around the house grumbling like a Japanese monster in a movie.

I re-read all the obedience books, and out came the chain choke. I was advised to lift her off the ground by this after aggressive outbursts. I tried several times. It became clear, I could have killed her and she would not back down. When I threw her in her crate, she turned and showed her teeth. I could not believe with the good temperament of both parents this could happen. Perhaps it was bad combination of hair-trigger reflexes of the Ibizan and bull-headed tenacity of the heeler?

After six months of this I decided on the final solution. We loved Fcasco, but obviously at the rate we proceeded, someone was going to get hurt. It was very difficult, but I was so sure it was the only possible decision. So we had her destroyed.

Then the evil spirit seemed to transfer to Ashley! *She* started fighting and physical correction made her surly. She never bit me, but she warned me when I slapped her under the chin or shook her. It started to look to me like something was deadly wrong here.

Many things about traditional dog training have bothered me, gone against the grain so to speak. Recent years have brought many positive changes, but when a problem arises most books and training institutions still go back to strong physical corrections. It appears to work with many, but some dogs are too soft or too strong-willed. The strong-willed ones often become labeled incurable or genetically defective. **These are really often the best dogs.**

I read every new animal book that our wonderful library acquires. There it was, the *"Jelly Bean Book"*. It sat here on my table for two weeks before I finally got to it. I was intrigued by the Dr. Jekyll and Mr. Hyde image set forth. Ironically, we had started to call Ashley psycho-dog due to her erratic behavior.

I read the book from cover to cover, and it totally turned me around in my thinking. Without detailed instructions, just by not using dominate training methods and changing my attitude, I found it worked. Taking Ashley firmly by the collar and saying, "no," putting her near me and praising her lack of aggression her fighting stopped! Soo-Simple!! But of course, Ashley is a very smart dog. All tension settled at feeding time. I was again able to feed everyone of my dear companions from their own bowl at once in the kitchen.

By showing the dogs clearly what I wanted, praising good behavior and simply not allowing the bad, now peace reigns in our home again. Ashley is again the good canine citizen, keeping the livestock in hand and helping to catch chickens on command.

Unfortunately, my ignorance resulted in the loss of a much loved and superior dog, it cost Fcasco's life. I had tried my best. I never intended to harm my dog, but as the saying goes, "The road to hell is paved with good intentions." This was a tragic experience. If I can assist Bill Meisterfeld to prevent future tragedies and regrets, perhaps it was worth it.

Nan Kilgore Little
Rustburg, Virginia

SHERRY

What a pleasure to read a book like *Jelly Bean vs....*that finally made complete sense about the inner workings of a dog's mind.

I have purchased and ordered over fifty dog books on behavior and training. I also bought a book on wolf behavior to better understand dogs. There is no comparison. You have dispelled a lot of misconcepts and beliefs of all the other authors....Yes, your mutual respect philosophy is the only way to train.

Sherry Poole, Poole's Dog World
Aberdeen, Maryland

SHARON AND SPREE

Just three short months ago I considered placing my dog in a new home or even having him euthanized.

For the first two years of his three year life, I had been using traditional dominant training methods. The result was a non-trusting, fearful dog.

Now, after only ten weeks of psychological training and repro-gramming my dog is becoming a trusting, willing companion.

I know this method is right, and the results are truly amazing. I am so grateful that never again I will have to use traditional domination methods or be a part of turning a trusting companion into a fearful schizophrenic!

Sharon Newman and three year old Great Dane, Spree
Blacksburg, Virginia

P.S. I am bonding with Spree for the first time and the bond is getting stronger every day.

CAROL AND COMPANION

I am so happy to have found C.W. Meisterfeld's book *Jelly Bean versus Dr. Jekyll and Mr. Hyde*. I found this book really amazing and just couldn't believe that it explained to me why I was having problems with my dog, a Standard Schnauzer. I've bought, borrowed and been given over 20 books dealing with dog training and behavior. All of them instructed me that the only successful way (success is what I wanted) to train my dog was to use the alpha roll-over, the famous shake can, the scruff shake, the scream at the top of the lungs to get his attention, and for housetraining to rub his nose in his mess and then throw him out the door (which I did not do and still have a totally housetrained dog), so he would know that is where he was supposed to do "it".

Well after reading *Jelly Bean vs...*, I found out that the negative training methods I had used were the reason why my dog became disobedient, untrustworthy, very dominant in expressing and exercising *his* will, instead of mine. Thus, I had destroyed everything I had aimed for, an obedient dog.

I paid a lot of money for my dog and wanted to train him the best possible way. I was told that my dog behaved this way because he was going through adolescence, or, because he was an unneutered male, or because he was of bad breeding, which I knew couldn't be true because of the research I did about his pedigree before I ever got him.

My dog would even chase the children around and snap at them, which I was told was because he just wanted to play. But my children didn't appreciate being bitten by their pet. I wondered if I would eventually have to keep them away from him totally, which would have defeated my purpose of getting him.

I was thankful to C.W. Meisterfeld for having opened my eyes to the truth.

I started training him with mutual respect and only the positive training methods he described in his tapes. I have already achieved positive results. My dog now sees me as his master instead of his equal or subordinate, and we are really starting to work as a team now. He obeys and even let me groom him the other day, which entails stripping his coat since he is a show dog. I was delighted to be able to groom him without fearing that he would turn and snap at me, which he had done previously.

I look forward to having an obedient, trustworthy companion and family pet after I finish the training course from C.W. Meisterfeld's tapes.

I can see now that the problems did not result from bad breeding or adolescence, or from being unneutered. Without doubt, the negative training methods I was so faithfully using had turned my family dog into a loaded gun waiting to go off.

I do hope that many, many more dog owners will find this book and realize that their family dogs are waiting for them to train them with mutual respect, so they can perform their duties out of respect for their owners, not out of fear, which is all we are doing to our dogs when we throw a can at them or scream at them, or shake them. How would we feel, if someone did that to us? It would scare the pants off of us and we would stay away from that person. That is what we are doing to our poor canine friends, we're scaring them into doing what we want, but as soon as we're out of sight, they will do what they want anyway. One day that accumulated fear will cause them to explode and turn on one us, which will lead him to the pound or being put down. All this can happen, because they are not trained with mutual respect.

So I do hope that just as my dog and I are starting a new life through the mutual respect, master-dog relationship, many more dog owners will benefit from being a real friend to their dogs by training them in a humane way by just giving them due respect!

I plan in the future with Mr. Meisterfeld's assistance to set up my own training school, so I can help many more people to really enjoy man's best friend.

The best to all of you and your canine friends.

Carol Williams
Crestview, Florida

CHRIS AND INNIS

I totally agree that physical correction does more harm than good. But after reading an article in a popular dog magazine on How to Train Your Puppy, I have a hard time determining the non-physicality of scruff shakes, or of the fear induced by use of the rattle can or other loud, obnoxious noises. These methods of correction are just as physical as hitting a dog and can as readily destroy a dog's temperament.

How would a parent feel about these methods if they were used to help teach children in school? Hard shaking of children has been known to produce severe brain damage (see the article "Protect Our Children" in the March 18, 1990 edition of *Parade Magazine*). A dog's brain is no more protected than a child's, and the possibility of damage due to hard shaking is just as strong. A mother dog does indeed correct very young puppies with this method, but she does it very gently, and the practice is replaced by verbal reprimands as the puppies grow up. Have you ever seen an adult dog discipline another adult dog in this manner? What would happen if a wild animal trainer tried to discipline a full-grown Bengal tiger by shaking it by the neck?

Psychologists and educators have long acknowledged the ineffectiveness of teaching children by inducing fear. Rattle cans and loud noises interrupt an undesirable behavior, at least at first, because they induce fear. Then, one of two things happens. The dog can be so traumatized by the fear that he avoids the situation entirely in the future, and you have started on the path to producing a shy, fearful dog; or he becomes accustomed to the noise, and the degree of correction must be continuously escalated to remain effective. It is easy to see that it would not take long before the noise can no longer be increased and the correction loses its effectiveness. Furthermore, all the dog has learned from these methods is that he cannot trust you not to hurt or scare him, and at that point you have a dog that you cannot trust either.

I know whereof I'm speaking. I raised a dog according to the guidelines of the dog establishment, taking him to a puppy kinder-garten class, using the recommended rewards and corrections, and treating him like a member of the family. I am a 5 ft., 1 in. tall woman, who weighs 117 pounds, and it was pretty frightening to have an 80 lb. male German Shepherd attack me without warning. Thankfully, I escaped serious injury, but I was devastated that this had happened.

Where had I gone wrong? I was told by an animal behaviorist that he probably had a genetic defect. I was afraid that I would have to have him put to sleep.

Shortly thereafter, I ran across a book with the title *Jelly Bean versus Dr. Jekyll and Mr. Hyde*, by C. W. Meisterfeld. This book was the first book I had found (and I had read many, many books on the subject) that explained the possible consequences of using dominant correction methods like the scruff shake, rattle cans, noises, and the alpha roll-over. Instead, C.W. Meisterfeld recommends the prevention and elimination of problem behaviors by building up a dog's respect and trust in the owner using only positive reinforcement.

I am a graduate student in psychology, working on my doctoral thesis, and thinking about his methods, I began to realize that they are based on sound psychological principles.

With his help, I am now in the process of reprogramming my dog to be a loyal, obedient, and happy companion, one who trusts me and whom I can trust in return.

I can't emphasize strongly enough how important it is for dog owners and trainers to begin to re-examine the dominant training methods that have been so widely disseminated recently. Their effects can be seen in the ever increasing incidence of dog attacks on people, and the ever increasing number of dogs being put to sleep because of behavior problems.

I realize that these methods were designed to help prevent these exact problems, but the simple fact remains that, for many, many dogs, they *just don't work*. Once this is understood, then we can begin to train our dogs in the more humane and effective manner that they deserve. Our lives, as well as those of our dogs, will be enriched as a result.

Chris Biggins
San Francisco, California

AS NATURE INTENDED

The day Jethro decided to lunge at the stranger in the hallway I knew we needed help. It seemed that he was indeed the "spooky, unpredictable" Mastiff the obedience trainer warned us about. I had

205

followed her advice and training methods to the letter, so why did I have the feeling that the next lunge would be accompanied by a bite?

My consultation with Bill Meisterfeld two days later gave me an explanation I was not prepared for. What follows is my understanding of what is going on inside the head of my dog Jethro and thousands of other dogs. Please learn from my mistakes, they may save your dog's life.

Upon the advice of a local veterinarian, I had read C.W. Meisterfeld's recent book, *Jelly Bean versus Dr. Jekyll and Mr. Hyde*. I began to see that some of Jethro's problems were discussed in this book, and I thought that it might be helpful to take him in for testing and evaluation. We dropped him off and returned to hear Bill's recommendations four hours later.

Jethro's deep psychological problems had two specific causes. The first problem was humanization, caused when a dog is treated as if he were human. The second problem was fear, a by-product of negative training methods.

Humanization is a condition which is created by the owner of the dog. The problem results from not having a strong master-dog relationship and catering to the dog. When catered to the dog is put in charge and never needs to develop servitude.

This is not a natural state of mind for a domesticated dog. In the absence of servitude, the mind of the dog remains undisciplined, and with an undisciplined mind, many other states of mind are developed and nurtured only to surface in any number of unpleasant and surprising ways.

A dog develops fear as a result of negative training methods. Negative training methods work on suppressing the dogs will-to-power, rather than cultivating the will-to-serve (servitude!). Dogs have an innate trust and respect for mankind. This trust and respect is destroyed by training methods that require pain and punishment techniques.

If a dog is treated with trust and respect rather than admonished with pain and punishment, it will maintain the trust and respect for mankind that it was born with. The will-to-serve will naturally overrule the will-to-power. Trust and respect are what make the domesticated dog a companion animal. Pain avoidance techniques, along with the many other negative training methods reduce the domesticated dog down to the wild animal behavior level. The survival instinct takes over because the dog is operating on fear, not trust and respect or servitude.

After hearing Bill's explanation of Jethro's problems, I became very angry. I was angry because at that point I knew that I had been led astray by the obedience trainers I had worked with for over six months. Right from the start they taught me techniques that destroyed trust and respect. They conditioned me to condition my dog emotionally. The weak master-dog relationship I had with Jethro was reinforced by the emotional conditioning techniques I had picked up at the training classes. I learned to give indulgent, gushy praise continually. This can best be described as the "Love 'em Up, Beat 'em Down" kind of hype we used in every class. It goes like this: the dog performs well so charge him up, then start the next exercise. To get the dogs to perform again, you must "beat" them down, get them to shut off all the excitement. This is usually done with some stiff jerks and loud No!'s and a chin slap or two if necessary. This type of "praise" leads to emotional dependency and schizophrenia, not to devotion and servitude.

The product I had created after six months of obedience training was a 165 lb. Mastiff that was both emotional and temperamental and operating on his survival instinct. He was both afraid of me (due to negative training methods), and afraid to be without me (due to emotional conditioning and continual catering). Was it any wonder that his behavior was starting to become unpredictable? My behavior to him was unpredictable, as he never knew what was coming next, praise or punishment.

How could we "undo" the damage we had done? Bill then explained the "reprogramming" process. It was possible to eliminate the former behavior pattern by establishing a new relationship with the dog. Nurturing the new relationship would reinforce a new pattern of behavior. The old pattern of behavior would fade in time and the dog would return to normal. He also explained that 85% of all behavior problems can be eliminated this way, just through the encouragement of a new pattern based on trust and respect, and servitude, and not reinforcing the old pattern of behavior. Like grass, if it's not watered, it won't grow.

After four months of reprogramming a new behavior pattern was instilled in our dog. Also, we gave our "new" dog the new name "Dumplings." The hardest part was not for the dog, but for us, his owners. We had to learn new behaviors also, because Dumplings would take his behavior cues from us. If we remained the same people, he would have remained the same dog with the same attitude he had before. We did no longer cater to him, and let him decide what's next on the agenda. We became his masters and treated Dumplings like a dog. This is the relationship nature intended, the dog a companion for man and man a master for the dog.

Now, after an additional four more months of conditioning with respect and trust, it has become possible to take Dumplings out in public, participate in AKC shows and breed him, if I so desire. Last July these things would have been impossible because he was a "dangerous dog," due to improper handling methods taught to me and my husband by an AKC member obedience club instructor.Our dog is not a specimen of poor breeding or mentally unfit. If he were, the rehabilitation would not have been successful. He was a victim of the current trend in obedience classes - "get tough with your dog" and really show him who's boss, through negative training methods.

Now Dumplings is friendly, obedient and happy. I'm his master and he doesn't bear the burden of being in charge anymore. But, the entire rehabilitation was *unnecessary*! This dog and others like him should never have been subjected to the negative training methods! Without the negative training methods this dog would never have gone into the survival mode and tried to lunge and bite.

He never will again though! He's very solid and secure, and sees the world through the eyes of a dog, not an undomesticated "wild" dog fearing for his life.

My suggestion: Don't subject dogs to pain avoidance and dominant fear techniques. Thus they will have no reason to bite anything smaller or weaker than themselves. Only trust and respect bring out the true companions we all want.

Janet Ziedrich
Healdsburg, California

Author's Comment

Because Janet was interested in the welfare of other dog owners and their pets she personally contacted the local institutions asking if they could visit this particular training classes which she had attended with her dog to observe the methods taught. Neither organization was interested or offered any help. She then met with a county supervisor. He recommended that she should obtain names from other dog owners with similar experiences resulting from the training classes.

So Janet placed the following ad in the local paper: "If obedience training messed up your dog like it did mine, we should talk, phone..."

The dog training club responded by holding a hearing and expelling her from the club. All because Janet disagreed with the abusive, dominant training methods and wanted to help other unfortunate victims.

I feel, this is a grave injustice done to a person caring about other people and their dogs. She deserves our respect and admiration.

VI.

DISCIPLES' CONFESSIONS

BRIAN

My name is Brian Coyne. I am a dog trainer in San Francisco with approximately eight years actual training experience in San Francisco and New Jersey. Above all else in my life, I have loved dogs as far back as I can remember. I felt closer to dogs than I did to most people. Also, I was able to express myself to them which I could not to most people. They have been there for me when it seemed no one else was, especially after my mother died when I was only eight years old. Dogs have never been afraid to show love and affection.

My story is one of the most painful experiences in my life. I am sharing it hoping to prevent that other do owners will make the same mistake, for their own sake and for the sake of their dogs.

Almost one year ago I received a call from an acquaintance who is a professional dog walker in San Francisco. The employees of a store where she was shopping had found a stray pit bull (without any identification) playing in traffic. They had tied the dog up in front of the store awaiting pick up by the Humane Society.

Judy knew the policy of the Humane Society. The dog would be kept for a short time and if the owner did not claim him, it would mean his destruction.

She sized him up to be a sweet, playful dog and made a decision to take him home. However, her husband did not want a pit bull in the house with another dog and a cat. Therefore, Judy was calling around to find a home for the dog.

It was about three weeks after my oldest dog had died of cancer when she called me. I really did not want another dog. But I thought, if nobody wanted him, I should take him and do the best I could. I wanted to save him from getting into the wrong hands or from destruction. I knew what it felt like not to know where to go or to whom to belong. I had experienced that when I was 15 years old after my father had died. I projected my own feelings onto my new dog.

"Bunky" was the name I chose for him. When I got him, he had a punctured eyeball. It was an old injury. The vet had no idea how it actually had happened. I had to spend approximately $250.00 in medical costs until it healed properly. Another problem arose upon bringing Bunky home, when my roommate refused to live in the same house with a pit bull. He moved out, which meant that my rent doubled. The reason I mention this is only to explain the daily stress that we bring on ourselves trying to hold things together and not realizing or admitting it, and ultimately hurting ourselves and others.

This meant that I had to work more and had less time to put into Bunky's training. He was both a physically strong and willful dog. Because of his breed and my lack of history on him, I was very apprehensive about his ability to be around other male dogs. I was always afraid to allow him to mingle freely. I always kept him leashed. Once, when I walked him in the park, he was attacked by three male Golden Retrievers. They bit him on the leg and ear and released him only when their owners came and got them off.

I held Bunky's head to prevent him from protecting himself, because I was afraid if he bit the other dogs, he would be blamed and ultimately destroyed.

Wherever I was with him, it seemed that I always had to be on guard and watchful of every situation. I believe Bunky became just like me.

During this time I taught Bunky how to "heel," "sit," "stay," and "down" on command. He performed willingly to all commands in controlled environments but was not very willing to "stay." In my opinion, it was not lack of intelligence but lack of willingness. I began to take this personally.

Everything I had ever been taught about training said, you have to practice more and become more forceful. Looking back at this time in my life, I became abusive to this helpless creature that I professed to love. I destroyed any respect and trust that I was hoping to develop in our relationship.

There were times, when I had group training sessions and put Bunky on a "down-stay," that he would begin with play manipulation. He would start to roll over and then proceed to get up. I would always correct him. These corrections became more and more forceful as the months went by, with alpha roll-overs, scruff shakes, and a lot of direct staring into his eyes. Sometimes, I am ashamed to admit, I would lose my temper and self-control and hit him.

I found myself using methods I had never agreed with but was so frustrated and desperate that I used them anyway.

The result in the end was the *exact opposite* of what I had hoped to accomplish. One day, after he had lived with me for nine months, this smart, playful dog turned on me. I can honestly say today that he had every right to do that. I actually unintentionally had taught him to do exactly that.

During one of these group training sessions suddenly an unleashed neighborhood dog came running into the circle of dogs in the class. Bunky got up and ran toward the dog. Because I was afraid he would harm the dog, I grabbed the leash, pulled him back with all my strength, and began to shout at him. That was when he turned on me. I was lucky to prevent that he got me. Then I was able to talk him back into a state of calmness.

I was scared and very ashamed that he had attacked me. I knew then that his behavior would be unpredictable and probably dangerous. I realized I had ruined my dear companion. I had been destroying everything good in that dog by forcing him to live in a constant state of alert, progressively getting worse putting him on the level of survival with no other option than flight or fight.

That very afternoon I took that at one time beautiful, loving dog and had him killed. I will never forget that day. It was a turning point in my life.

I could not let him die alone. I held him. He did not want to die and I did not want him to die, but I did not know what else to do. I felt that I should be the one on the table being destroyed and not him. This was the nightmare I will never forget.

What happened afterwards I will always remember. I couldn't sleep, I couldn't look anyone in the eye, I felt like a criminal and the biggest failure in the world. I really just couldn't bear the thought of living, I didn't think I deserved to.

I contacted at the SPCA in San Francisco a grief support counsellor for people whose pet died. I had met Betty almost 10 months before when my oldest dog died. That was my first step in asking for help.

I knew that the problem was not with the dog. It was with myself, my decision to use the training concepts that are taught all over. I realized that these methods are dangerous and abusive and can not only destroy the relationship of owner and dog but can be fatal, in most cases for the dog. Because I loved dogs so much and I did not want to be instrumental in their destruction, I decided that I would never own or train a dog again. I felt completely lost, drained and incapable. I felt like a nothing.

This is the human being I brought to Bill Meisterfeld. A completely broken person that didn't know whether he was salvageable or even worth the try.

It was during our first conversation that he told me, the most important and essential step I must make is to forgive myself. He recommended to start by never repeating that same behavior again. He offered, if I was willing to learn, that he would be able to teach me.

I will never forget these caring, forgiving, hopeful words. I knew in my heart I was not a bad person and never meant to create the situation I had experienced.

C.W. Meisterfeld has changed my life forever. He gave me a new vision of myself and all other living creatures in this world. He taught me how to relate to them and to understand them, especially dogs, in a way that I was never taught before. To have a communication with them that only develops respect and trust, where there is no room for anger, punishment, and fear. For that I love him and will always be grateful. He taught me not to be judgmental, but first of all to accept and understand myself. In doing so I can help myself and others who want help.

I am now a graduate of the Meisterfeld Psychological Dog Training School. I am back into teaching group classes and private clients Bill's unique philosophy of training dogs with pleasure, not pain to either to the dog or the owner.

Brian Coyne, MPDT Graduate
San Francisco

KATHI

Darby and I now have a master-dog relationship which is great. Before I thought I had a good relationship with my dogs but now I know the difference. I really didn't train much as far as stand, sit, down, stay. My puppies were just trained for grooming coats. With bait I taught stand and stay. At seven weeks I would personality test, then lead-train and start taking them out in the front to socialize with children. They were kept in our dining room so they heard all the kitchen noises.

Everything I read was yell at the puppy if it was doing something wrong. Usually my yell was outside, if the puppy had an accident in the house. I set up a playground in the backyard, a big box for them to run through, a chimney flu, ladder and a tire. They seemed to have a lot of fun and I had less fighting. They had plenty of chew toys, squeaky toys, stuffed toys, etc. They loved to play with milk bottles with the tops off, and aluminum cans with both sides off.

At the young age of six or seven weeks Darby began to back away when I approached him. He had a very outgoing sister who was always the first to come. We at that time considered him cautious. He always did what I wanted, but I now realize he was withdrawing into himself. When loud noises were made he went outside. He wasn't tolerating his environment as well as I thought he was.

Darby slept on our bed, along with his mother after he was housetrained. I humanized him by treating him like a little child. He received very little training. Since I was told to keep them together, he stayed with his mother.

When I groomed him, I laid him on his side to file his nails and also to blowdry him. I now have a command, "play dead," for these activities.

The rest of Darby's case history was already described. Therefore, I will continue the story after I picked Genghis (the new Darby) up from Bill Meisterfeld.

Bill had taught me how to work with the dog, to heel, stand-stay, sit-stay. Since I was afraid I'd mess my dog up again, Bill also worked with me on being non-emotional, non-judgmental.

Brought home, Genghis stayed outside in a run. Rugs were put over the fence, so he couldn't see the pool. He was kept in a controlled environment with as little chance for fear responses as possible. I was his only human contact. I trained him 15 minutes four times a day. I really made a commitment to my dog. When I was training him, I practiced being in the here and now, concentrating on my dog. I did not permit other thoughts to interfere, since he would notice it immediately and goof off.

For three weeks I worked just on the heel, stand-stay, and sit-stay. Then I started the psychological dog training workshop with Genghis which lasted eight weeks. During that time Genghis began further to improve. He was less shy. His will-to-power began to increase. His tail was now up more and more.

Then I changed his name back to Darby. During the eight week of class I decided to let him sometimes in the house. It was a real learning experience to see his old program coming up again.

I returned him to the back yard again on a full-time basis. I was really learning patience!! I always knew, he would one day be fine. I was determined to do everything I could to reach that end. He started being fearful of some things again. This was 90% acting, an interesting behavior. "I'll stay shy if I want to," he was saying.

When Bill offered a workshop again, I went for another eight week period. During that time, I took Darby downtown, exposing him to all kinds of situations and socializing him. Sometimes, he would revert right back to his old program. Lack of trust leaves a deep imprint. Therefore, I returned him to the controlled environment. I was now training Darby 30 minutes twice a day. There was a big change in Darby around the fifth week of the second workshop. His tail was up most of the time. If he reacted to some-thing, he would come right out of it. I learned not to respond to his unwanted behavior. Thus, he had no reinforcement for negative behavior. I continued to train Darby in the back yard according to Bill's instructions.

A month later we had a one day workshop. Now at 15 months Darby was wonderful, tail up and wagging, just like the puppy he should have been. I could have cried and jumped with joy, but I've learned to control my emotions around an animal like Darby. During our class that day we all trained the other people's dogs, and Darby showed no fear with any of the others who handled him.

Darby and I are still training in the back yard and further developing his trust and loyalty. His will-to-serve and his will-to-power are becoming balanced. It took me a while to learn to understand my dog, while he knew me in 1/44 of a second.

I have changed, my dog has changed and the results are absolutely terrific!! I plan on doing conformation and obedience trials, and anything else I feel like doing with this dog. All this became possible, because I developed his mind, his will-to-serve.

Thank you, Bill, for being here when Darby and I needed you. The training you have given us saved both our lives.

Kathi Stidwell, MPDT Graduate
Castro Valley, California

LISA

I started showing and training dogs about four years ago.

It all began with my first dog, an American Staffordshire Terrier named Sable. I took her through a local obedience class. With my second dog, I began to get interested in competition obedience. I started to show and attended more obedience classes in our area and in other places. The methods I was taught sometimes seemed a little too harsh, but being a novice, I did what I was told.

Every method I have applied in the past was always based on total physical domination over the dog. I have used hard jerks and pulls for heeling, the alpha roll-over, ear pinch, hard jerks on the choke collar as a correction for offenses, yelling and slapping. I have also used prong collars on my dogs. My dogs responded to this type of training with fear and stubbornness. They ignored my commands, were non-trusting, and sometimes even would challenge my authority.

This is not to say that we did not do well in the show ring. We have received many high scores in obedience trials, First Place ribbons,

Second Place ribbons and other good scores, but the quality of each performance varied from show to show.

As time went on I continued to train, but I always kept looking for a better way. I thought, in order to be a really good dog trainer, I needed to be able to understand the way a dog thinks and to know why dogs behave the way they do. When I met C.W. Meisterfeld and learned about his training philosophy, I finally found what I was looking for. His training technique works with the dog and his way of thinking, not against it.

I have used Meisterfeld's approach on my own dogs and dogs that I have rescued from the local animal shelter. I have had nothing but success using his methods. I have a puppy that went from being hyperactive and destructive to being passive and well behaved. The dogs that I rescue are often neglected and abused. By using these techniques on them I have produced dogs that are trusting, happy and well-behaved pets for their future owners.

I also give classes teaching this system to my students. All of my students have been very happy with the positive changes in their dogs. They are also very pleased having achieved these changes by training their dogs in a humane way based on mutual respect, instead of using harsh corrections and physical domination.

The results I have seen using C.W. Meisterfeld's philosophy have proven to me that this is the only way to train a dog. The outcome is always the same, it produces a happy obedient, trustworthy animal.

Lisa Scherer, MPDT Graduate
Napa, California

SHELLY

Over the past ten years I have experimented with several different methods of dog training. These methods ranged from dominant fear-producing techniques to bribery with baby talk and food. All these concepts produced counter-productive emotions in the animal and trainer. For example, the "Alpha-Wolf" methods, which are used by many professional trainers, force the dog to be submissive. One of the ways this is being achieved is by rolling the dog on his back and glaring into his eyes until he is no longer struggling to get up. The owner practices to be the dominant "pack leader" as if he were a dog himself.

Dog's were brought into the human structure to work for us and protect us. Therefore, it is important to have the proper relationship, the "master-dog" relationship, where the owner is in control and not the dog.

This relationship can be achieved practicing C.W. Meisterfeld's philosophy of psychological dog training. I am using his system in my training classes and have found it to be very effective also with my own puppy. At the age of 12 weeks he was jumping up and trying to bite all of us. When he succeeded in knocking down my two-year-old daughter, he would try to bite her in the face.

What really amazed me on my first day as a MPDT student was, when I asked Bill Meisterfeld what I should do about Chase's biting, that he answered, "Nothing, just begin to develop his will-to-serve-and-please." While Bill explained this to me, Chase was biting on his legs. Bill's answer was so different from the instructions in the books and from other dog experts who advise you to cause pain to the dog or scream, when he bites, in order to let him know that this is wrong.

Well, within 10 days Chase stopped jumping up and trying to bite us or knocking down my daughter. He was beginning to show respect for my family. All this was accomplished without pain and punishment.

Dogs trained with psychological methods have no fear of their owners and yet are very attentive and willing to perform. The owners are happier because they are getting results without using any force or bribery. They frequently comment that their dogs are calmer both at home and in the training sessions. By not being jerked, yelled at, or hit, the dog's survival instinct is no longer triggered and he can relax. Now, the owner is in charge as the respected master but not as the feared top dog.

Shelley McDonald, MPDT Graduate
Rohnert Park, California

Dr. Meisterfeld's Canine Psychology
Home Study Course
"Sharing 44 Years of Professional Dog Training Experience"

Start your own unique career opportunity teaching obedience classes and training other people's dogs with the most effective, natural and humane technique on earth! Dr. Meisterfeld's home study course provides you with the tools and the knowledge taught at his 4 day workshop. This Home Study Program is ideal for those who can not travel to Petaluma, California. Learn natural, holistic training techniques (at home) for all phases of dog training from puppies to rehabilitation of problematic dogs. Solutions for some of the most difficult behavioral problems are addressed, including fear, viciousness, separation anxiety, psychosomatic illness and rage syndrome.

The following audio tapes, video tapes and books are all included in this special package.

AUDIO CASSETTE ALBUMS
#1 Canine Behavioral Psychology   4 Cassettes
#2 Psychological Dog Training   4 Cassettes
Full all-day seminars taped at Sacramento State University.

VHS VIDEO "CANINE CAPERS"
"Sir Walter" (costume dog) helps trainer humorously demonstrate how improper obedience training causes behavioral problems. Great for prepping your obedience class on "How to Train Without Pain." This video comes with non-commercial public performance permission.

BOOKS
1) *Crazy Dogs & Crazy People: Looking at Behavior in Our Society* **by C.W. Meisterfeld and Ernest Pecci, M.D.**
2) *Psychological Dog Training: Behavior Conditioning with Respect & Trust* **by C.W. Meisterfeld**
3) *Tails of a Dog Psychoanalyst* **by C.W. Meisterfeld**
4) *Jelly Bean vs. Dr. Jekyll and Mr. Hyde* **by C.W. Meisterfeld**
5) *As a Man Thinketh* **by James Allen**

"SPECIAL EDITION" #1　　　　*Rage Syndrome Study*
VHS Video　　　　　　　　*by C.W. Meisterfeld*

This case study shows how to prevent and how to cure Dr. Jekyll and Mr. Hyde (Rage Syndrome). The video is a documentation of a dog considered unrecoverable by America's top dog behaviorists. The only solution recommended by others was to destroy him. Filming starts from Day 1. Watch this dog transform from a highly dangerous dog to a completely rehabilitated, safe and trustworthy pet. Throughout the footage Meisterfeld shares his unique training principles founded on mutual respect. You will be truly AMAZED as you view the transformation without any use of negative correction/reinforcement or drugs! Since 1963 Meisterfeld has saved approximately 3,000 problem dogs with very challenging behavioral problems, including many with "Rage Syndrome." Some of these dogs have killed other dogs, cats, deer and sheep prior to their rehabilitation.

"SPECIAL EDITION" #2　　VHS Video
The Unique Nature of Man's Best Friend Rehabilitated Pitbulls
by C.W. Meisterfeld & Lisa Sherer

This video helps destroy the myth that American Pitbull terriers are highly dangerous animals and cannot be trusted, particularly with children. Lisa Sherer, a graduate of Meisterfeld's School, demonstrates how pitbulls (rescued from her local humane society) who were formerly trained to fight, can be reprogrammed to become nonaggressive pets. Lisa shows you the commands and principles which transform the dogs into adoptable family pets that are 100% safe around children. With the Meisterfeld training philosophy, these pitbulls lose their aggressiveness to the point they will not harm strange animals that accidentally trespass on their territory. **All this was accomplished without any form of negative reinforcement, prong collars or drugs!**
These Editions are worth the cost of the whole program!

Meisterfeld & Associates
448 Seavey, Suite 9
PETaluma, California 94952
Tel: (707) 763-0056 ● Fax: (707) 763-1539

OTHER BOOKS BY C.W. MEISTERFELD

Jelly Bean versus Dr. Jakyll & Mr. Hyde was written for the SAFETY of our CHILDREN and the WELFARE of our DOGS. It explains how the dog's mind works and what dominant training methods cause behavioral problems. It includes 16 pages of full color photographs and graphs.

$19.95 Hardcover, plus $4.50 for postage/ packaging.

Crazy Dogs & Crazy People is a unique combination of psychiatrist and canine psychoanalyst sharing their experiences and understandings of the neurological, psychological and emotional similarities and parallels between human and dog.

$26.95 Hardcover, plus $4.50 for postage/ packaging.

Please note, when both books are ordered, only $6.00 postage is required.

MEISTERFELD'S SCHOOL OF
CANINE BEHAVIORAL PSYCHOLOGY &
MUTUAL RESPECT BEHAVIOR MANAGEMENT

TWO UNIQUE WORKSHOPS IN ONE

This integrated four-day workshop is presented at Meisterfeld Ranch Kennels. The principles taught in these workshops can be applied to *all phases* of dog training such as: simple home obedience training, A.K.C. competitive training, competitive field and water training, and problem dogs with a variety of neuroses including rage syndrome. You will be working directly with C.W. Meisterfeld as he personally teaches and instructs this philosophy along with some "tricks of the trade" which are only taught in his workshops. The unique combination of these two workshops is based on Meisterfeld's 35 years of experience in working with thousands of inter-relationships between dog owners and their dogs and with people inter-relating with other people.

WORKSHOP 1: CANINE BEHAVIORAL PSYCHOLOGY
You will be taught how to psychoanalyze and rehabilitate problem dogs with: separation Anxiety, Hyperactivity, Fear and/or Shyness, Aggression and Rage. You will receive specially designed charts and personal instructions on how to keep a daily record customized for the particular problem dog that you brought to the workshop with you. Your dog will also be psychologically tested by Meisterfeld before training begins.

WORKSHOP 2: MUTUAL RESPECT BEHAVIOR MANAGEMENT
You will learn the nine basic principles of human relationship behavior which will enhance your working with dog owners and in teaching your obedience classes. You will discover that these principles are very beneficial in day to day living both at home and work.

For more information please write to:
Meisterfeld & Associates, 448 Seavey, Suite 9
PETaluma, California 94952 or FAX: (707) 763-1539

INDEX

C

D

E

F